Vic's Big

from SW France to NW England

Vic Heaney

To Chris

Thanks for your support

All proceeds go direct to pancreatic cancer research

Photographs can be seen online at:
https://picasaweb.google.com/vicngay/VicSBigWalk02

Best wishes

Vic Heaney

Vic's Big Walk ISBN 978-1-4717-3035-1

Originally published as an electronic book by Vic Heaney and BookBaby

Copyright © 2011, 2012 Vic Heaney

The right of Vic Heaney to be identified as the author has been asserted.

All rights reserved. Except in the case of brief quotations quoted in reviews or critical articles, no part of this book may be used or reproduced in any manner whatsoever without written permission of copyright owner.

Cover design and photograph by Peter Labrow
http://www.labrow.com

For Gay.
I could not have done any of this – the walk or the book – without you.

Contents

Chapter 1	*Day 1:* Puivert to Mirepoix. Letter from Nicola. Why am I doing this?
Chapter 2	*Day 2:* Mirepoix to Salles-sur-l'Hers. Early planning.
Chapter 3	*Day 3:* Salles-sur-l'Hers to Auriac-sur-Vendinelle. More on preparations and training, dangers on the road.
Chapter 4	*Day 4:* Auriac-sur-Vendinelle to Lavaur. Problems with my foot. More background.
Chapter 5	*Day 5:* Lavaur to Salvagnac. More background. Protection from dogs. Dr Barbara Moore.
Chapter 6	*Day 6:* Salvagnac to Penne. Pancreatic cancer.
Chapter 7	*Day 7:* Penne to Caylus. Trees.
Chapter 8	*The Second Week:* Caylus to Milhac-d'Auberoche
Chapter 9	*The Third Week:* Milhac-d'Auberoche to Persac
Chapter 10	*The Fourth Week:* Persac to Allonnes
Chapter 11	*The Fifth Week:* Allonnes to Sougé-le-Ganelon.
Chapter 12	*The Sixth Week:* Sougé-le-Ganelon to Mutrécy.
Chapter 13	*The Seventh Week:* Mutrécy to South Stoke
Chapter 14	*The Eighth Week:* South Stoke to Atherstone
Chapter 15	*The Ninth Week:* Atherstone to Wilmslow
Chapter 16	*The Tenth and last week:* Wilmslow to Blackpool

Chapter 1

Day 1. Puivert to Mirepoix. Letter from Nicola. Why am I doing this?

I step onto the Voie Verte, the old railway line between Lavelanet and Mirepoix in the Languedoc area of the South of France. I have walked 10 kms since I started out at about 8 this morning. There are only about 1,990 kilometres left to go.

My objective is to reach the house where I was born, in Northern England, in 70 days time. This will be exactly 70 years to the day after my first appearance there. I am walking back through my life, from my home near the Spanish border, to the very beginning.

This is something that has been in the planning, preparation and training for 2 years. It is a massive undertaking and I only hope that I can achieve the objective. My initial plans were to do the walk quietly and unobtrusively and not tell too many people about it. But that changed when I decided to raise money for charity. Obviously publicity is likely to increase donations so I have maximised the exposure as much as I can.

In Puivert, the small French village in which I live, people have gradually become aware of what I am doing and a small crowd turns out this morning at 8 o'clock to see me off. Most of them accompany me for the first kilometre or so. Among them is my wife Gay, who will now lock up the house for three months and leap into the motor caravan which is our back-up vehicle and our home for a while. I will meet her again at the end of today's walk.

Some time ago an old friend suggested that the start would involve bands, speeches, roars of appreciation and acclamation from the crowd. On the day, there are no bands or speeches but there is some cheering. Things have moved on a bit from the original idea to slip quietly out of town. It is touching to see that so many people have dragged themselves out of their beds to see me off.

During the first 10 kms, two people from the village catch me up, one on a bike, one in a car, to wish me well, which is kind. That is when I am walking on roads, but for the rest of this first day's walking, to Mirepoix, I will be on the old railway track where there is no traffic allowed and in fact where I rarely see people walking or cycling, which is a shame because that is what the track is for.

This chemin de fer existed to service local communities, to bring in raw materials and take away the finished goods. Although it is now a splendid resource for walkers and cyclists it is sad to see that it no longer exists as a railway. I say this not as somebody who has any nostalgia for railways as such, but because all the towns that I pass on this track have lost their industry, which is why the trains no longer run. The first town I pass is Chalabre. Here they used to make everything for people to wear – they could dress you from head to foot – hats, shoes and everything in between. Now nothing is made here. The weekly market in Chalabre used to stretch all over town, in various streets. Now you are lucky if the Saturday market can muster 10 stalls. That is obviously a sign of the disappeared prosperity of this town, which is clearly a sorry shadow of its former self. The same applies to several of the smaller communities which I pass during this first day's walk.

As I walk past the extensive apple orchards of Sonnac sur l'Hers a runner comes towards me, going at a good pace. He is wearing a huge beret. As he approaches he shouts, "Good luck, Vic, see you in August". I met this runner only this morning. He is a journalist who was outside my house at 8 this morning to cover the start of Vic's Big Walk for the Independent and the Midi Libre newspapers. He says we used to run in the same races when Gay and I were competitive runners. He has also seen me out training for this walk but today was the first time we had a conversation and, blow me down, here he is again a couple of hours later.

I emerge from the second of the railway tunnels – fortunately both have lighting installed – and find myself crossing a bridge high above the road at Camon. Camon offers itself as a miniature Carcassonne and includes the old Abbaye Chateau which has been renovated and is now a splendid hotel and restaurant. It is a bit of a stretch to compare Camon with Carcassonne, which is a stunning, complete, mediaeval walled city.

I have never seen this track as muddy and wet as it is today. I walk the Voie Verte regularly, although never before in this direction – I have saved that for today. Almost every week I walk from Mirepoix to home (34 kms) on this same route, as part of my training. I have used it at all times of the year, including midwinter, but I have never seen it in this condition. Yet we are five weeks from the high point of summer. This morning the weather started out reasonably fine, although clearly it was never going to be warm. The maximum temperature forecast was 11 degrees. I don't think it has reached that.

Most of the old stations along the Voie Verte have been converted into houses. Everywhere there was a station, there is now a placard telling you something about the village the station served and the products which were made there.

One of the communities I pass is Lagarde. There is a Chateau of Lagarde, dominating the landscape a couple of kilometres away. The placard informs that it was often referred to as the Little Versailles of the Languedoc. Although it looms over the surrounding terrain it is more or less a ruin. It is allegedly under restoration with the prospect of returning it to its former glory, but from where I can see it there is no sign of any work. Nevertheless, it is a dramatic sight.

Other communities with informative signs I pass along here include Moulin

Neuf, which used to be a water-milling centre, producing flour. There was a railway turntable here, which is where my route turns sharply left and another branch of the railway – I am not sure whether it is now used as a track – swings right to Bram.

As I reach Roumengoux, very Italian-looking on its hilltop, which is 6 kms from my finish in Mirepoix, it starts raining heavily.

I feel a bit tired after the first 25 kms or so. That doesn't sound a good omen for 70 days walking, but during training I have already experienced that some days one feels good, other days, for no apparent reason, even on the same route, one feels weaker. I think it is called being human.

Today is one of the longer sections I will walk. I am trying to average 30 kms a day. This leg is 34 kms. Most of my stages are planned to be about 30 kms, some are more, and I am trying to ensure when I have done a "more", I try to do a shorter one the next day to even things up. This is not always possible because the terminus of each day's stage is really dictated by where there is a campsite – ideally a campsite close to the tracks I will walk.

Lots of trees have fallen down over the track in the past few days, making it quite difficult to negotiate. I don't know how cyclists manage. Unusually, there is a group of cyclists about today. They keep going off the track to explore then reappearing. They have passed me three times and have learned more about my project each time.

Some of the trees are broken and some are completely uprooted, the whole tree falling over. I think this is a result of the ground being so wet that the root system is weakened, which makes the trees susceptible to the high winds and snow we suffered last week (May!).

I arrive at Mirepoix feeling fine if a little tired, but have I bitten off more than I can chew? What will it be like walking like this for 70 days, without a rest? Like most older people, I am not really aware of my age. I feel no sense of trepidation. Maybe my mind is protecting me from being aware of what a mammoth task this is. I was stunned to receive this e-mail yesterday from my daughter Nicola.

Dad,

Only one day to go. I think I must be feeling much more emotional and agitated than you are. Or than you seem to be, anyway. I have spent the last few days with tears in my eyes at the mere thought of what you are about to undertake, and I'm sure YOU haven't been going around with tissues in your hand!! ...

... the thought of all the energy and effort, both mental and physical, you are about to put into such a mammoth task would be worrying for any daughter of a soon to be no longer 69-year-old man ...

There was much more.

Gulp! Nicola is a very level-headed person, not given to dramatics. She seems to be horrified at what I am doing and clearly fearful of the outcome.

What am I doing, and why?

It all started with a few simple words.

"I've had an idea!"

Gay looked at me as if to say, "Oh dear, what is it this time?"

Previous "ideas" have resulted in us both giving up well paid jobs, going to live in France; then to spending the winters abroad – first in Cyprus, latterly in New Zealand. We were in New Zealand when I had this latest revelation. Some may think it an odd place to be inspired with the idea of a long distance walk from Southern France to Northern England.

In March 2008, we were staying in Alexandra. Each morning we walked along the Central Otago Rail Trail to Clyde. For me this walk had another objective, rather than just getting some exercise. The old Post Office in Clyde is now a café and restaurant. Their date scones are some of the best in the world. The café opens at 10 a.m. so we made sure to be on the doorstep at that time, so that we could both have a drink, I would have a date scone (Gay, being more sensible, having had breakfast before we set off), then we would walk back from Clyde to Alexandra along the banks of the mighty Clutha River, blue water from the glaciers, powerful and roiling despite being constrained by the massive Clyde dam. The round trip is 26 kms. Other more casual walking later each day brought the total to over 30 kms.

We kept this up for two weeks, alternating the direction of the daily walks, and an idea began to form in my head. Until then I had found walking very boring. A competitive runner all my life, I had recently been forced to give up my sport because of a knee injury. I had been in the habit of running 40, 50 or more miles per week. When the running had to stop, I found it very frustrating to walk even 4 miles because it was taking me 3 times as long to cover the same distance. Now with an objective – the splendid scone and coffee – what a simple soul I am – I was enjoying the walking, despite each trip taking four and a half hours. There was beautiful scenery, something to aim at, and a sense of achievement because, after all, the walks were pretty long.

That is part of what gave me the idea for Vic's Big Walk. We had walked over 400 kms in two weeks. This fact was gelling with other thoughts already in my head.

Throughout my life I have read mainly non-fiction books. These included many accounts of people doing long-distance walks. I remember the tremendous coverage given by press and television to Dr Barbara Moore as she walked from Land's End to John o'Groats in 1960. Long ago I read John Hillaby's Journey Through Britain and have since read several other books about people doing that same trek in one direction or another. Others have undertaken walks that are more personal to them. The Sea On Our Left is about Shally Hunt and her husband walking around the coast of Britain. More recently I read The Man Who Broke Out Of The Bank And Went For A Walk In France, in which Miles Morland and his wife tramp from the Mediterranean to the Atlantic, averaging, as it happens, 30 kms per day. I thought that if this really unfit couple could do it, so could I, although I would prefer to pick my own route. So even before the inspiration in NZ I had already thought that I would like to do a long distance walk some time but needed a point to point which was significant to me.

Quite separately I had also been wondering what to do to celebrate my upcoming 70th birthday. Most of my other big birthdays have been marked by dramatic changes in my career or lifestyle. At the age of 20 I had already ditched one "safe" career as a Merchant Navy officer. By 30 an even safer Civil Service job had gone. At 40 I left a well paid and established career with a computer manufacturer. At 50 I severed connections with the then thriving company which I had founded at 40. When I was 60 I celebrated by throwing the only birthday party I have ever had, and was living in a foreign country. What to do for my 70th?

While doing the scone marches in NZ I began to think again of doing a significant walk, then I thought of possibly connecting this to the 70th birthday. The Eureka moment came when my mind leapt to a very specific walk which would be absolutely unique, I knew nobody had ever done it before or would probably do it again. I would walk, setting off on my 70th birthday, from the house where I was born in Blackpool, to the house in Southern France where I now live. This would take me, in 70 days, along the journey which, at the first attempt, had taken me 70 years.

My feeble brain gradually realised that Plan A would have me on the roads of France at the busiest and hottest time of the year. I switched to Plan B. I would set off 70 days before my birthday from my home in France, so that I would arrive, very symbolically, at the house where I was born, on my 70th birthday.

I would walk backwards through my life, from the present to the beginning.

I told Gay what I was thinking of doing. She supported the idea, although she did point out that 70 days on my own did not sound like something I would enjoy. That is true. I am not a man who enjoys long periods of his own company. I would of course like Gay to accompany me on the walk but she was silent on that score. A few days later she said she would come with me.

I tried the idea out on some friends, partly to clarify the ideas in my own mind and to talk through some of the snags. The response was most encouraging, although this is when I was first asked whether I was going to walk across the English Channel or to swim it. I soon perfected the groan that question produces.

By the time we arrived back in Europe I was referring to the walk as Vic's Big Walk or just VBW. Most comments from friends were encouraging, but I'm not sure about this one, "It's a most original way of spending a 70th birthday but then you were always a bit off the planet - in a nice way of course".

Or from another friend (after I had mentioned the difficulties Gay and I, as vegetarians, would face eating away from home in France) . "Don't be such a wimp Wickers! The veggie Yogis of India have walked barefoot from Kerala to Rishikesh or the Kumbh Mela [and back] for centuries, negotiating the odd Tiger along the way. Honey, sunflower seeds, nuts, dates, figs, milk, water, juice …"

Having told so many people, I was now committed. But why was I doing this? I was born 23rd July 1940. So on that same date in 2010 I would hit 70. A walk of 70 days seemed an obvious idea, once I had thought of it. Obvious symbolism – 70 years of life, 70 days walking. 70 years getting to where I am now – 70 days to reverse it. The distance covered would be somewhere between 1700 and 2000 kilometres, depending upon the exact route chosen.

Why? I wanted to do something memorable (for my own memory, that is – I don't expect it to go down in the history books) to mark the occasion and to celebrate the fact that at what used to be regarded as an advanced age, I am luckily still fit and healthy. I had been thinking for a while of doing something to celebrate my arrival (I hoped) at my 70th birthday in a reasonable state of repair. Vic's Big Walk was now that something.

I also wanted to do something which would give me a sense of achievement and which would give me plenty of thinking time to dwell on the long journey from then to now.

I started a blog on the Internet (http://vicsbigwalk.blogspot.com), the aims being to receive comments, advice and help, not only from family and friends but also from anybody else who strayed onto the blog and who felt they had something to contribute.

A great deal of planning had to be done. Also a lot of thought about the perils and pitfalls, the roads and routes, the accommodation, the feeding and watering, whether this would be for my own satisfaction alone or if I should use it as an opportunity to raise funds for a good cause.

Chapter 2

Day 2. Mirepoix to Salles-sur-l'Hers. Early planning.

It's half past seven on the morning of 16th May. I am leaving the wonderful mediaeval centre of Mirepoix behind me. This place will surely become a UNESCO Heritage site one day, if it can negotiate the politics which must be involved. The spacious market square is a riot of half-timbered, brightly coloured buildings. The wooden gargoyles alone, on one building, are a great attraction for photographers, which, in these days of the mobile telephone, means almost everybody. Walking rather than the usual driving out of town, I have seen several splendid old buildings which I haven't noticed before.

From here on the trip is entering terra incognita as far as I am concerned. I know the route to Mirepoix very well, but now it will be all new to me, walking-wise, and for the most part I will be in places I have never clapped eyes on before.

For the next four days I will be walking on roads, which is something I would rather not do, but it takes me to a sensible joining point on the Grandes Randonnées system, an immense 160,000 kms network of walking tracks throughout France. Although Gay planned this part of the route meticulously to make sure the roads were as quiet as possible, we also drove over the route a few weeks ago to make sure they were safe for walking. But where I am walking today, and from here to Normandy, I have never walked before.

I leave the café where I had my breakfast and said goodbye to Gay, I have gone less than 50 metres when I realise that the koala from my hat is missing. I go back and it is lying forlornly on the pavement outside the café. This could have been a disaster. A friend in Alexandra gave us New Zealand badges to carry with us, one of which is on the front of my hat, the other one Gay has, to remind us throughout the walk that our friends in New Zealand are with us all the way. Then our Ozzie next door neighbours and friends, while giving us a farewell dinner, provided us with tiny clip-on koalas to remind us of that our Australian friends are also with us during the trip.

It's quite a pleasant morning. Again, it is not going to be very warm today but at least there is some sun in the sky. It's a bit windy – I have to hang on to my hat as I walk over the River Hers. We have a River Hers and River His in this area and as most French rivers have signs at the bridges, giving the river name, this makes for some very interesting photographs – she standing by the His sign and he propping up the Hers.

At the extent of the Mirepoix city limits, instead of following the busier main road to Fanjeaux, I turn left and then immediately right into a very narrow road which, during our recce, we found to be remarkably quiet.

I am walking in bright sunshine but there are very black clouds ahead so clearly the weather could change at any moment. I have a very serious retina problem (pattern dystrophy) as a result of which I am going to completely lose my central vision. There is nothing that can be done about it but there are a couple of precautions I can take. I should eat lots of Omega 3, which "might" slow down the rate of deterioration. Also, at all times when it is sunny, I should wear dark over-glasses over my specs because the sun is very damaging to my retina problem. I have the over-glasses at the ready in a case attached to my backpack.

This road is proving to be an excellent choice. It is hillier than expected, even though we have previously driven this way. Modern cars don't tend to notice hills, whereas legs are more sensitive. There is some traffic but maybe an average of one car per two kilometres. All I can hear most of the time is the sound of the birds, including woodpeckers and cuckoos. Yesterday I heard some bee-eaters as I walked along, and I have already heard some today. Yesterday they were quite low. Unfortunately I could not make out their plumage, which is a shame because they are such beautiful birds

I have a rear-view mirror to use when walking along roads but on a quiet road such as this it is not necessary because I can hear an approaching car for some time before it reaches me.

As I pass a magnificent modern looking building up on the hillside, with huge amounts of window, a goat wanders down onto the road to greet me, then follows me along the road for half a kilometre. I fire up my anti-dog taser-like device, ready to give it a burst – the taser, that is, not the goat. Not to touch the taser to the animal, or hurt it in any way, but because the taser makes a fearful sound which would hopefully make the goat go back. I don't want to be responsible for leading somebody's pet goat to Blackpool. It's bad enough that I need to go there myself. Fortunately the animal must have received my telepathic message because at this point it stops walking, bleats pitifully, and trots reluctantly home.

I arrive in the small village of Lafage after walking for 13.5 kms rather than the 11.5 kms I have on my notes from when Gay and I drove the route – I don't know what has gone wrong there. I turn right down the charmingly named Route des Anciens Combattants, then onwards and upwards.

On my iPod, in addition to music I have many hours of Michel Thomas language courses, both French and Italian, to study during the next ten weeks of walking, but not for the first few days while I am on roads. Safety is obviously the most important thing here. I need to be totally aware of any traffic approaching. So I have plenty of time to reflect on the past two years of preparation and planning.

On the D325 I pass over a wonderful narrow, humpbacked, mediaeval looking bridge, with a view dead ahead of a very large building – one of the type which my Italian ex-son-in-law used to call a "stately" – a large stately home or chateau. I never find out what it is because, as I approach, I turn left onto the 102.

At La Remise, where I turn right onto the D625, I take out the magic banana, a well-known refuelling food, much used by cyclists on the go. Before I set off this morning I drank, as I will every morning, a third of a litre bottle of beetroot juice. A recent discovery shows that this extends the performance of endurance athletes by about 16%, so it is now part of my daily intake for Vic's Big Walk. I feel a bit like a battery in the Duracell adverts.

After another 34 kms day (would I have walked so far without the beetroot juice?), I pull into Salles-sur-l'Hers, where Gay is waiting with V-Force One, our magnificently decorated campervan.

—

Gay and I did not consider for very long the idea of carrying large rucksacks and tents and cooking equipment together with food supplies. My back has several flaws – I know what triggers them off and usually manage to avoid any problems but when I get it wrong things can be really bad. The rucksacks, et cetera, would be inviting disaster, so instead of carrying our home and kitchen we would be seeking accommodation each night and eating out much of the time. This would raise problems of its own.

We are vegetarians. Two thirds of the walk would be through France. The French do not generally understand the concept of not eating meat. We have had some splendid meals here in restaurants where the chef rose to the challenge. More often we have come up with a blank. Some places have even refused to make us an omelette. Not to mention that, magnificent as French omelettes are, we would not want to eat one every night. No, food and sustenance would be a big problem for vegetarians in a land of much splendid food, hardly any of which is suitable for freaks such as us.

We began to give some thought to the idea of using a motorcaravan. This would solve at a stroke our problems of accommodation and food. Obviously the camper would be our accommodation. It would also let us carry and prepare our own food. It would mean that we could carry far more in the way of changes of clothes. We could even carry my guitar and Gay's keyboard and so keep up our music practice. I could take a computer and keep my blog up to date each day. I could write a book!

There were two big snags with the campervan plan. One was that we did not own one. The other was that someone would have to drive it. Unless we wanted to spend 70 days in a confined area with someone else (and we did have a kind offer from a friend, to be our driver), it would mean that Gay would become a driver rather than a walker. She was very keen to walk.

It struck us that, although motor caravans are very expensive, we could buy a used one and then sell it again at the end of the trip. It would probably not cost much when offset against the alternative cost of hotels and restaurant food.

Friends made various creative suggestions but these inevitably raised other snags. The horse drawn caravan, the donkeys, mules and llamas were attractive ideas but would slow us down, not to mention that animals, like humans, get sick, and tired, and sore.

Another friend suggested that we use the UK Vegetarian Society to contact vegetarians along our route with a view to them putting us up for a night. He also suggested that the Veg. Soc. could be more interested if we used this to publicise the benefits of vegetarianism, especially its impact on the environment (costs many times as much to produce meat, gas emissions from animals, et cetera) but I was not sure I wanted to be the centre of that sort of publicity. There was also the possibility that it could provoke the type person who wants to argue or attack anybody seen as different in any way.

We sadly came to the conclusion that, alluring though the thought might be, of walking with a llama or donkey, the snags, allied to those of accommodation and food were such that we would be using a motor caravan. Gay would be the driver, except maybe where we could get volunteers to drive a stage for us so that Gay could walk with me. Sad but true.

There were clearly many other points needing much thought. Was it a good idea to walk every day for 70 days? Could the body stand it, at 70 years of age? What would be the ideal route? Would we need, or be able to arrange, back-up and support?

In vague terms, I wanted to walk from Puivert to Normandy, say Caen/Ouistreham, take the ferry to Portsmouth, then walk from Portsmouth to Blackpool. In France, that would be a shorter trip for us than using one of the Channel ports. In UK, it is more pleasant to walk (or drive) up the West side of the country than the East, to avoid negotiating London.

For the French leg, the intention was for me to use the Grandes Randonnées, walking trails which criss-cross France. We got the maps out one night and were delighted to see that the GR36 runs all the way from Caen to near Carcassonne, which is 50 kms from home. A connecting GR runs through Puivert.

But then we got down to distances and were dismayed to find that by walking up the GRs, the distance in France would be 1600 kms, compared to about 900 kms by road. Not only would it be a lot further (because the GRs wiggle about a lot) but the distance would be much too great to accomplish in the 70 symbolic days I had set for the whole trip, including England. So it was back to the roads. Quiet roads, I hoped.

With our running and racing background Gay and I know that it is folly to indulge in strenuous activity every day, without giving your body rest days and a chance to recover. I wasn't sure whether this also applied to walking. If I walked 6 days then rested on the 7th (could I start a religion here?) it would mean only 60 walking days, which would probably not be enough.

There were many suggestions, from people following my blog, that I should use the event to raise funds for a charity. I had mixed feelings about this. I realised it could do some good, but it could also put me under pressure to achieve, whatever the circumstances of weather, illness, injury or other unforeseen problems. I had noticed that these days most sponsorship is attracted and paid through the Internet and is paid in advance. How would I feel if I had a lot of sponsorship paid up and then for some reason I was unable to complete the trip? As conceived, the project was for my own satisfaction – that would change.

Recently, my daughter Karen had completed the Manchester to Blackpool (60 miles) sponsored bike ride, an annual event which hundreds of people enter to raise money for their favourite charities. Karen raised funds for the Hospice in Blackpool. She had very personal reasons for choosing that beneficiary. Her mother, Gaile, my first wife, died of pancreatic cancer. She was treated in a hospital in Blackpool, but her final days would have been spent in the Hospice if there had been a place available.

What about publicity? I had conceived the walk as a private project, for my own satisfaction. Of course, if I chose to raise money for charity, it would be a case of the more the merrier and one way of boosting it would be to maximise publicity.

This could involve informing, and hopefully coverage by, local – possibly national – newspapers, as I progressed along. Played to its maximum – and if a 70-year-old man walking back to his birth was interesting enough – it could involve radio and television. Did I want that? As with the fundraising, there was much to think about.

Chapter 3

*Day 3. Salles-sur-l'Hers to Auriac-sur-Vendinelle.
More on preparations and training, dangers on the road.*

As I leave town at 7 a.m. on Monday morning, everywhere in Salles sur l'Hers is closed. There is a bar/restaurant, which was also closed yesterday, a boulangerie, a shop, a tabac, a bank which is only open two mornings a week. Everywhere is closed. No coffee and croissant to start the day.

After 4 kms I come to St Michel-de-Lanes, which seems to be very pleasant. I have done those 4 kms on a busier road, the D25. Busy for France but it would be regarded as a very rural road in Britain. Now I am down to a single track road as I leave St Michel. This is the D43d, which is virtually traffic-free.

After just over 9 kms I reach a five-way junction, where I turn right towards Avignonet, site of several éoliennes, wind generators. As in other countries, in France there is much opposition to these – of course they are a good thing, but should always be elsewhere. I find them to be fine, I have no problem with them at all. As my brother Paul says, they have their own beauty.

Soon I find myself walking parallel to the Canal du Midi, but only for a few yards before the road swings right and crosses the canal, a magnificent engineering achievement which crosses France from the Mediterranean to the Atlantic. It was built in the 17th century, a long time before the canals in Britain. Like most continental canals it is substantially wider and takes bigger boats than the British canals. I have never understood why British canals are so narrow, when the precedent was already there in Europe for wider. I would love to be able to walk along this canal, because at least it is flat, which is more than can be said for the rest of today's route.

Very soon I cross a bridge over the busy Autoroute des deux Mers, which also crosses from the Mediterranean to the Atlantic. I'm glad I'm not walking along that. In less than a kilometre I come to the railway line which I suppose is also the East-West route. As I approach the crossing, the barrier comes down and I have to wait as a train whizzes by, although it is not one of the incredibly fast TGVs.

I plough on, up hill and down dale. There seems to be rather a lot of up, although the countryside here is more rolling than the dramatic contours of the Pyrenees, which I have left well behind now.

I am walking along mainly quiet two-lane and some one-lane roads with virtually no traffic.

I go through places with names like Les Hucs, En Raou, Lamis, la Desirade. Then onto the D72 to Belesta, through Mourvilles-Haute.

Entering Le Vaux, I see 3 windmills within 100 metres, all ruined. I photograph another one coming out of Belesta. At least that one has the remnants of sails. These windmills are ideally situated, judging by the way my hat blows off.

Leaving Le Vaux, I have about 8 kms left to go. I am hoping that some of them will be flat, because this has been a hard day, the third one of well over 30 kms, and probably the hilliest so far, constantly up and down. While hills make things more interesting, they also make harder work.

I am to be disappointed in the sought-after flatness. The hills continue, but eventually I drag my battered legs into Auriac-sur-Vendinelle, where I see the welcome sight of V-Force One where Gay has parked it in La Place de la Republique, as agreed with M. le Maire during our survey trip several weeks ago.

This turns out to be another place where our "Internet Everywhere" dongle from Orange does not work. It is rapidly becoming known as "Internet Nowhere". We had a very poor signal in Mirepoix but managed to put a posting on my blog and deal with some e-mail. Then nothing in Salles or here. I promised people I would try to blog every day, but if the facilities are not there, what can I do?

The walk was without incident but was, unfortunately, 36 kms, which means that I have walked a total of 104 kms, instead of 90, in the first 3 days of VBW. I could do with a shorter stage soon. I am averaging well above the 30 kms a day I set myself, which in itself is pretty demanding.

—

I have had several offers of company on various legs of the walk. I have accepted very few. I have no objection to some company some of the time, although I look forward to plenty of solitude and thinking time – after all I have to plan the next 70 years of my life.

When I walk with others, there will be difficulties of scheduling and arranging the start of each day's walk. I start very early by most people's standards. And they will have to walk at my pace. Our American friend Lorenzo Minor, when he and his wife Janie stayed with us for a month and walked with me a little, could be heard vehemently saying to people, "Do not walk with this madman - he will kill you!" I walk at about 6-7 kms an hour and my objective is to get to the other end in the shortest possible time so that the rest of the day is free.

Also there is the problem of accommodation. We seem to have sorted out our own accommodation now we have acquired a battlebus, but I am sorry, we are not willing to share it of a night time. Especially with the hours we are keeping, early to bed and early to rise, which would not suit most people.

Several friends made approaches to motorcaravan manufacturers. The objective was to find a company willing to supply a vehicle for the duration of the walk. Unfortunately, by this time the recession already had its teeth in the legs of economies, companies had been badly hit, and these approaches came to nothing.

In any case, I don't think this type of sponsorship is as easy to find as is generally supposed. I heard Dame Ellen MacArthur, the famous round-the-world sailor, being interviewed on the radio. She said that before the big ocean races which made her so famous, she wrote hundreds, or it may have been thousands, of letters to companies she hoped would sponsor her.

'And how many replies did you get?' asked the interviewer. 'Not one,' was her reply. The point she was making was that companies are constantly being asked to sponsor people and will only go for the already well-known. Or sometimes those for whom they have a personal introduction. Dame Ellen would have no trouble getting sponsorship now, of course.

We looked at secondhand campervans and saw nothing to our liking, so we decided to have a new one. We have owned two campers in the past and thoroughly enjoyed using them. Perhaps during this trip we will get the bug again and decide to keep it. Clearly if we decide to sell it after VBW we will lose money, but this would be offset against all the hotel bills we will not be paying.

Of course, at the same time as all this pondering and planning was taking place, I entered serious training. In the walk itself I would have to average something like 30 kms a day. It would be folly to go at that rate during the two years of training I had before me. The result would most likely be injury and an end to the whole project before the official start date. I started on a carefully planned build-up. Gradually I increased the distance walked per week so that by the end of 2008 I was frequently walking more than 100 kms per week.

Most of the walks were on country tracks, including some locally which form part of the network of Grandes Randonnées. During one of my Wednesday morning walks from Quillan market to home, I decided for a change to walk along the roadside, rather than on one of the GRs which goes almost parallel, where I normally walk. At this stage I seemed to have abandoned the idea of doing Vic's Big Walk off-road, because the distances were unattainable. I thought I had better experience roadside walking before I committed myself to 10 weeks of it. Like most country roads, there is no path at the side. In some cases there is a ditch, or something else, such as a crash barrier, preventing one from seeking an escape route if the oncoming traffic (I was walking on the left side of the road, against the traffic) is coming too close. Most of the oncoming drivers pull out a little, to give some clearance, but it is surprising how many do not. Don't they realise that a slight stumble – perhaps caused by their alarming proximity – could cause a disaster? To themselves as well as the pedestrian?

So constant concentration and preparation for escape are needed. But the bigger problem is with traffic going in the same direction as the walker. You would think that as they are on the opposite side of the road, there is no danger. But when the road ahead is clear, i.e. no traffic coming towards me, the overtaking happens. On that one 16 kms walk, I had several cars and vans almost brushing my shoulder. They just made no allowance for the fact that for some reason I might deviate from the straight line. All very alarming, and yet there is no warning of their approach.

I got to thinking that I needed some sort of a rear view mirror. I had occasionally seen the little mirrors which attach to cycling helmets. Would one of those, attached to the peak of my walking hat, do the trick? I quickly acquired one and attached it to the peak of my cap for a trial. A trial which failed. It was virtually useless to me. It was very difficult to align it so that I could see behind and to the right of me, then it moved at the slightest touch, so that it was no longer aligned correctly. The instructions that came with it said that it could be tightened with an allen key but I'm damned if I could see where. Its other major failing, although this may be one of mine, was that my eyes focused beyond it. It was too close to me.

Wearing this device on several road trips, I never managed to see a car approaching behind me, which is what it was for. It was a bit of a talking point, though. Several people asked me what it was, although I would have thought it was pretty obvious. We bumped into our doctor in Chalabre. He said, "What is this?" I'm afraid that it was only later that I realised I should have told him I am a dentist. So, to add to its other failings, it did not sharpen my wit.

I realised that the main item of safety equipment required was alertness, and it would be vital to pick roads which were as quiet as possible, as long as their selection did not increase the overall distance too much.

However, dangerous traffic continued to exercise my mind about the best way to have a rear view. I toyed with the idea of designing a device something like the contraption which Bob Dylan used to use to hold his harmonica while his hands were occupied with his guitar. I found a supplier of "dirty old men walking sticks", which turned out to be a stick with a mirror attached. I bought a clip-on mirror to use with my own stick, should I choose to carry one. But then I found a better answer to the problem.

I don't know how many of you have heard the expression "fifty shilling washtub". An old friend of mine said his mother used to refer to people this way if they were a little broad in the beam.

That is as may be, but what I found was a fifty cent mirror. I bought it at a vide grenier, or what is known to Anglo Saxons as a car boot sale. It is lightweight, plastic backed, convex, just like a car rear view mirror. It has a clip on the back, with a ball and socket connection, so it could if necessary be carried on a stick. But the socket folds flat and the whole thing is so light that it easily slips into my shorts pocket and, when needed, can be held in the palm of my hand so that I can clearly see the traffic behind me. Held at the correct angle, it is the answer to my problem. I don't know where it came from originally, but all walkers on roadsides should have one. It cost me half a Euro but the price of a new one would not be much, in exchange for a life.

As I walked more regularly, and for greater distances, than I had ever done before, my shoes were proving to be a very good choice. The particular type I was using were Columbia Trailmeister. Wonderfully comfortable, light, supportive and fairly hard wearing. Built almost like a running shoe, but with more sole and a stronger top. A shame they are not sold in Europe, but as we pass through Singapore and spend several months in New Zealand each year, I had a source of supply.

I had been using Trailmeisters for a few years. The only problem with shoes of this modern construction is that the soles are not replaceable. This is the price we pay for the lightness and comfort. I did have an earlier pair of Columbia shoes re-soled locally and they look fine, but they have changed character, much heavier and stiffer. I could even hear the difference if I walked in them. I use them for gardening.

One of the things I really like about Columbia, apart from their products, is their shining rebuttal of ageism. The company is run by 85-year old Gert Boyle. In Christchurch we noted that a Columbia shop had opened since our last visit. We paid it a visit. I flippantly asked the young man behind the counter how Gert was doing. He said that she was fine a couple of months earlier, when she had came from Portland, Oregon to Christchurch, NZ, to open the shop! Shall I remind you of her age?

Was I in full training for The Big Walk? I was asked this a number of times before the end of 2008. The answer was no. I did not need to be in full training yet, as there were still hundreds of days to go to the start. I didn't want to peak too soon, or to invite injury. No sportsman trains at maximum warp all the time. There is a gradual build-up, then usually a bit of a wind-down leading up to the event.

I always get plenty of exercise, normally a mix of walking, cycling, and – when the weather is against those two – a mixture of indoor rowing, indoor cycling and cross-country ski machine. So I was still doing a mixture of these things. But I was certainly walking far more than I had in the past. Strangely, although I had found that a 6 kms walk, as an ex-runner, was a slow, boring experience, I was enjoying far longer distances. Some days I was still cycling or rowing, but on walking days I was covering distances in the high teens (kms).

I kept up the mixture of exercise types for the rest of 2008. Then, from mid-January until mid-April 2009, as usual, we did a great deal of walking in New Zealand, over 100 kms most weeks, and lots of cycling as well. When we arrived home in May, I maintained, more than usually, the high level of walking. The aim was to do a minimum average of 10 kms per day, with at least one day per week of 20 to 30 kms. During the winter and spring of 2010 I increased my weekly distance walked to near-VBW levels. By the time the start date came round, I was fit and raring to go, with almost 12,000 kms of training in my legs.

As previously stated, the problem with walking as exercise, especially for an ex-runner, is that it takes so long! At least twice as long, probably getting on for three times, as covering the same distance with both feet sometimes off the ground at the same time. Walking 30 kms takes up a large part of the day.

My first 30 kms walk in France was after a dental appointment in Limoux, which is just that distance away from home, by the shortest possible route. I decided I would walk home from Limoux to give myself an idea how much walking time per day I should be planning for. I assumed 6 kms an hour, so expected to be home in 5 hours, which I was – to the minute. And that's with a climb from 180 metres to 680 metres, and in a temperature of 30 degrees Centigrade. I started the walk at 10.15, after leaving the dentist. Normally I would be on the road by 7 or 8 in the morning, so would escape some of the heat. But I would have to live with the climbing – France is a very hilly country. One thing I was very pleased with, and that was the amount of traffic. I was walking on a D-road. Most of the time I could not hear a car engine, and was without motoring company for minutes at a time. I had started to plan my route from home to Caen/Ouistreham, and hoped to be on "white" D-roads for most of the journey, so they would all, I hoped, be fairly traffic-free. These roads – which are coloured white on the map – are very minor, usually very narrow, and little used.

This first 30 kms walk, from Limoux to Puivert, was a strong possibility for the first leg of VBW – although in reverse. The other contender was Puivert to Mirepoix.

The route I was beginning to map out for the whole walk was more likely to take me in the direction of Mirepoix than Limoux. It was one of few stages which I knew I could do mainly off-road. An old railway line was recently turned into a walking/running/cycling/horse-riding trail from Chalabre to Mirepoix, which would account for most of the 34 kilometres of the day's walk. The track goes to Mirepoix without wandering too far from the road, so the distance is not much different and of course it is much safer and more pleasant. We had cycled it several times.

There were some unexpected side-effects of walking long distances in hot weather. The late great Hoyt Axton wrote and sang a song called "Bony Fingers" – he had a brilliant theory that this is what you get if you work your fingers to the bone. But now I discovered "Sausage Fingers". Gay and I both noticed it when we were walking a lot in Central Otago, New Zealand, earlier in the year. It must have happened before, but this was the first time it had struck us. I don't think it was just the heat. In the same time scale, we were doing a lot of cycling. So we were out in the same heat for the same length of time, with no sausage effect. On the walk home from Limoux, when I walked 30 kms in 30 degrees, I had a full load of sausages long before I arrived home. One day Gay and I cycled 60 kms with not a sossie in sight.

So it must be something to do with swinging the arms, blood rushing to the extremities, especially when in conjunction with the heat. Anyway, it was impossible to do anything dexterous for some time after the walk had finished. At my puny level of guitar playing, I found it impossible to finger the correct frets or pluck the right strings. If I was not trying to play fingerstyle I would probably have trouble holding a pick. In fact, that's the sort of trouble I have even before going for a walk, but this is not the time for me to cry in your beer.

Researching this nonsense at home I was amazed to find that I was not the sole progenitor of the phrase "Sausage Fingers".

A Google search on that phrase threw up 446,000 results! It is a recognised medical condition, and the phrase also has some rather unseemly uses.

If you search on "Sausage Fingers" and "Walking", there are 3,820 hits.

"Sausage Fingers" and "Guitar" produces 2,960 results.

And I thought walking would produce great thoughts?

Chapter 4.

*Day 4. Auriac-sur-Vendinelle to Lavaur.
Problems with my foot. More background.*

As I set out from Auriac at just after 7, it looks as if it is ramping up to be a very pleasant day. The sky has no clouds to speak of. It's been a very cold night but the forecast is for the temperature to be over 20 today.

I have a bit of a problem with my feet, or rather with one foot, which is rather galling – I have been telling people that I have walked 12,000 kms in preparation for this walk and that I have had no problems with my feet, therefore I am going to stick to the same type of shoes and socks that I have been wearing all this time. I am doing so but I made two mistakes. One is that I started the walk with two brand new pairs of shoes. I actually gave away some part-used shoes of the same type to a friend. I was convinced, after wearing these shoes for years, that new ones would not need any breaking in. But then, I have never before started them off by walking over 30 kms of mountainous terrain every day, for several days on the trot.

So I have a bruised toenail on my left foot, middle toe. I have always had trouble with that toenail – when I was a runner that was the one which would frequently bruise and eventually come off.

Second mistake was that after the bruising, I cut back the nail severely, so that it wouldn't be pressing against the shoe as much. I cut it back too far and the result is that I have a very swollen toe. Gay is very worried about it, and I'm not too pleased myself. But as long as it is only a bruise, it will subside and I will eventually lose the toenail – that would take months to happen. But I think I would like to know that it is not an infection because that could prove to be very nasty and be a threat to the whole walk.

Setting out at this time of the morning, even on these very quiet roads, I find them at their busiest. People rushing in both directions to work, and taking kids to school, of course. France is the only country in the world that I know of that has four rush hours per day, because most Frenchies still go home for a full lunch.

After a few kilometres I come to a sign off to a small hamlet. The sign says "Moscou". Clearly I am out of my depth, map reading wise, and well off course.

It's ironic that almost everything I am wearing, except for underpants and socks, is Columbia – even the rucksack – and the one piece of Columbia equipment which seems to be letting me down (I later revise this opinion and realise that my foolishness alone is to blame) – assisted by my own folly, is the pair of shoes of the very type which is the reason for my relationship with Columbia. I was so pleased with the shoes that I wrote to the company, eulogising. I wondered if they wanted to make any PR hay out of the fact that I had walked 1,500 kms in one pair of their shoes, without any problems of the feet. I was alternating two pairs of the same type, with a view to testing them to destruction so that I could calculate how many pairs I would need to cover the Big Walk. At well over 100 kms a week, it doesn't take long to get through 1,500 kms. I already had other brand-new pairs of Trailmeister waiting for a chance to strut their stuff.

It proved a little difficult to get through to the right people at Columbia, but once I made contact with Pascale Graffman and Nathalie Snowden, marketing managers in France and UK, things moved very fast. A teleconference was set up between the three of us and not only did they want to frame my shoes and exhibit them in one of their stores, but they were backing me to the hilt in my walking project. They would outfit me in Columbia clothes; they would have a link from the Columbia website to my blog; their PR companies would produce stories about me; and lots more. Pascale also said that when we acquired a campervan, Columbia would decorate it overall with a Vic's Big Walk design or whatever I wanted. It seemed that I now had a major sponsor. Not only that but Pascale sent me a copy of One Tough Mother, the book about Gert Boyle's life story, which I was very keen to read. They are lovely people to deal with, as well.

As a result they have supplied me with all sorts of clothing and my wonderful ultra-lightweight Mobex backpack – I received this 6 months before it went on sale in the stores and I can't recommend it highly enough. They have also paid for and designed the superb decoration of the vehicle, which includes, apart from their own logo, the logo of Satmap, my other sponsor, the Vic's Big Walk design and blog address. I should correct that by saying that they incorporated the Vic's Big Walk logo, which was designed by my friend Peter Labrow.

Columbia for the last few years have had a high-performing team in the Tour de France. Now they have me. And here comes my own Tour de France moment. I am walking along when a large vehicle covered with logos, many of which say Columbia, draws alongside and a hand reaches out, holding a drinks bottle, just as it happens in the T de F. Of course it is Gay, because I forgot to drink the magic beetroot juice this morning and here she is with it. She hands it over, we have a quick word, and she is on her way to do some shopping in the town ahead and to establish camp – and probably to look for a chiropodist.

At 8 kms I pass through Loubens-Lauragais. A steep climb up into the village centre, where there is a picturesque castle next to a church, with what seems to be the remainder of a moat between them, still full of water. I am seeing many places where I would like to linger a while with a good camera, but time's a-wastin' – must crack on.

Another windmill off to my right. I take a wrong turn out of Loubens. None of the road signs have road numbers on them, inviting confusion. So I spend longer than I intended walking along the busy and dangerous D826 before turning onto the slightly less busy and dangerous D42 for 400 metres. Then I turn onto the very quiet D35 to Maurens-Scopent, another wonderful name.

When I am on the hilltop between Maurens-Scopont and Veilhes, daughter Nicola rings me by arrangement. I have been unable to get an Internet connection through my dongle, to keep my blog updated. Hundreds of people per day are following my walk by reading the blog. I asked Nicola to ring me so that I could brief her on how to put an entry on the blog for me, a holding entry to explain to people that I am having this trouble and that eventually I will be putting a blog entry for each day that I walk, including the missing days.

I also receive a message from Gay to say that she has found an Internet place in Lavaur, but it closes from 12 to 2.30, so she will meet me in Lavaur at 11.30. Since I have 10 kms to go and it is 10.30, I have to decline the offer. Nevertheless Gay says she will wait in Lavaur for me and we can have a drink before I do the final 5 kms. She has also booked a campsite for the night.

Lavaur is a town of distilling, flour-milling and the manufacture of brushes, plaster and wooden shoes. More interestingly, it is a place of many eateries and cafes, one of which we give a bit of a road-test. While doing this, daughter Karen phones me from Saudi Arabia. I am not clear whether my hearing difficulties are caused by traffic in Lavaur or sandstorm in Riyadh.

This is the first time that I have tried breaking the walk up a bit instead of just charging on to the finishing post. I wonder whether the break will help or hinder me – whether rigor mortis will set in or if the rest will regenerate my legs. I find that the latter is true. Maybe I should not just set out and charge on for 30-odd kms without stopping, as I usually do.

The regeneration comes in useful because the last 5 kms from Lavaur are one very long climb – this has been a day of climbs – and while I am toiling up there Gay passes me and waits at a lonely 5-ways crossroads 3 kms from St Pierre. The climb is a worthy finish to a day of ups and downs, geographically. This junction was scheduled to be my 30 kms spot – as it happened it is 35 kms, so quite far enough for the day.

After she picks me up we go on past St Pierre where there is a beautiful old water mill, viewed from a narrow stone bridge, where I make a note to take a photograph the next day.

And so to a very rural campsite, which initially looks very dodgy as we drive into a farmyard and park in a field. There are proper hook-ups, et cetera, and a facilties block containing everything required. All is clean and tidy. There is even a washing machine, which enables Gay to catch up.

Gay is doing everything except the walking. She is a star.

Despite it looking so unprofessional, they have a colour leaflet extolling the virtues of their campsite and the area. We spend a very pleasant, very quiet night here. Not only that, Gay has acquired a USB extension lead so that I can dangle the dongle through one of the roof lights and I am able to get a signal, update my blog (although the signal here is still too weak to upload photographs), and catch up with e-mails (43 waiting – I give very brief replies to these). The extension takes the dongle outside the Faraday cage which the vehicle so proudly boasts to save us from lightning, but which probably helps to prevent bloggery.

Another long day of 35 kms. I have walked 139 kms since Saturday morning. But at last it was a really fine day, the first we have had for several weeks. It was pretty hard going again – one thing that is really being confirmed in my mind is that not much of France is flat.

—

A couple of days after my first 30 kms walk in France, I read that Rosie Swale-Pope had just completed a journey on foot which was far more epic than mine will ever be.

Five years earlier, she set off from her home in Wales to run around the world. The intention was to do it in two years, but in the event, she was away for five years. She arrived home with stress fractures and on crutches, but while away she conquered the freezing wastes of Siberia and Alaska, was hit by a bus, suffered from pneumonia and frostbite, and had a scare with breast cancer. Not to mention mad axemen and the like.

I have followed Rosie's exploits since she first hit the headlines when she and her then husband and two small children (one arrived during the voyage) sailed around the world in a small yacht. Of course the papers, being what they are, still talk of her as the blonde who "sailed around the world in the nude".

Headlines about Rosie now say "Grandmother runs … etcetera". I mused that press coverage of VBW would of course home in on the "Grandfather …" My granddaughter, Alexandra, would be 25 before I started the walk. How delighted the newspapers would be if she were to add another generation in the meantime so that they could be writing "Great Grandfather walks the walk." Of course I mentioned this in my blog to increase the pressure on her.

During the road walking which, during my two years of training, doubled-up as research, it was noticeable that on Wednesdays there was less traffic because there was no school run. At the time, various changes were taking place in the French education system. One was that they were moving onto a four-day week. Until then the kids had Wednesday off, but Saturday had been a school day, if only in the morning. You can imagine how that Saturday morning messed up everybody's weekend – it was very unpopular, but now it has gone.

They still have Wednesday off. The history of that is quite interesting. When church was being separated from state, just over 100 years ago, the churches obviously felt they were the losers, especially in the matter of access to young minds. So, as a sop, it was agreed that children would not go to school on Wednesdays and the churches could have them then (if they could catch them). This still applies.

Other days, there is a surge of traffic between 8 and 9 in the morning. So that is a time to avoid. I thought I would have to carefully plan each day, and each overnight resting place, so that I could start walking at 6.30 or 7, reach a strategically placed boulangerie and a cafe at about 8, stop, mange, drink, read the papers, ruminate, stretch, then set out again en route. I was hoping to finish each day's leg before lunch, or at least before the end of lunchtime (12 till 2 in France), for similar reasons. It is very common in France to have a bottle of wine with lunch. So the road is a more dangerous place in the early afternoon. It is very clear that many drivers are trying to improve their fuel economy – the number of near misses per litre (of wine) being the crucial indicator of success.

On my blog I was recording all these thoughts and developments, not only as a way of record keeping for myself, but to keep friends and relatives informed of how the project was developing from the initial thought, and to provoke comments and advice.

I had some spooky software which told me where in the world the blog's readers were. There was very good coverage in Europe and North America, Australia and New Zealand. I was also surprised but pleased to see several readers in India. The one that really delighted me was in Korea. I had been reading in the newspaper a theory that Kim Jong-Il, the strange leader of North Korea, had actually been dead since 2003. There was a long period during which he was not seen at all and there was speculation that any fleeting glimpses since then had really been a stand-in. But what if this theory was wrong? What if he was, instead, like much of the world, an Internet junky? Drugged by his Dell or Linked to his Lenovo? Transfixed by his Toshiba? Was he a VBW blog follower?

With all these readers all over the world I thought I had better tell them something about the region where I live, where Vic's Big Walk would start, why Gay and I live there and why we shall probably never leave. We have heard visitors use the word "Paradise" to describe it – a word we have heard used to describe only one other place, which is New Zealand, a country where we are privileged to also spend much time.

The area is absolutely soaked in history, mystery, and blood. The local newspapers recently covered an anniversary. It was 800 years ago that the Pope, in his wisdom, declared a crusade against the Bonshommes, the people who are known today as the Cathars. These were members of a peace-loving (sounds as if it should be the mainstream) branch of Christianity. The Cathars were in great numbers in the

Languedoc and were perceived as a threat to the Pope's own sect. So, in his wisdom, this (ironically named Innocent!) representative of the Prince of Peace decided to exterminate the Cathars and their numerous followers. He got together with the French king, who rather fancied the territory, because at that time the Languedoc was not truly a part of France. The crusade was designed to crush the Cathars and their supporters, and to integrate Languedoc into France. The military action went on for decades.

The Inquisition was invented at this time, in this area, for the express purpose of rooting out and burning Cathars. One rarely hears the word Inquisition without the adjective Spanish. But it was 200 years later that the Spanish merely used, against Jews, a tool which had already efficiently wiped out an inconvenient Christian belief. The operation went on for the duration of the crusade and for long after, until there were no Cathars left.

When I had set off from Puivert, and for long after I had lost sight of most of the town, lost in the tucks of the mist-shrouded Pyrenean foothills, I could still see Puivert castle, because the town, and our abode, stand in the shadow of it. So-called "Cathar castles" such as this belonged to local lords who supported the Cathars and tried to protect them (they were slain or dispossessed for their trouble). They are visible reminders of those terrible times, but what about the far more numerous invisible markers? How many of the steps I take through the Languedoc will cross the paths of marauding armies or fleeing defenders? How many scenes of ancient horror will I pass? How many unmarked graves or long-dead Inquisition fires?

If only the rocks could give up their secret witness.

At the time of the "Albigensian" crusade the Languedoc was one of the most prosperous and cultured areas in Europe, second only to Byzantium. The culture and the prosperity were destroyed by the Crusade and its aftermath, and the area has never recovered that position.

There are many more layers to the fascinating history of the area. There are still visible traces of the Visigoths, those sackers of Rome, who had their Western base not far from our home. There is the ongoing saga of Rennes le Château and the mysterious Abbé Berenger Saunière. There are many books and webpages about this subject.

All this in an area of stunning natural beauty, in the foothills of the Pyrenees.

Puivert is a village 50 kms south of the astonishing walled mediaeval city of Carcassonne. Together with its 10 or so satellite hamlets, Puivert has a total population of maybe 800. On some motoring maps you will not find Puivert marked. We are 500 metres above sea level. Our house was reputedly built by a drum major in Napoleon's Grande Armée. From one of our roof windows we can see the mediaeval chateau – 600 years older than the house. From our bedroom window we can see the plateau at 1000 metres, the Maquis du Picaussel, where 400 members of the

Resistance were camped out during the Second World War, supplied from the air by the Royal Air Force and able to see, from their great height, if the occupying German army were approaching. That did not help the village of Lescale, a little lower down the hill, which was destroyed by the Germans in their frustration.

There is a huge amount of visible history in the area, in spectacular settings. The roads are quiet, the weather is generally kind, without the stifling heat and humidity often found at lower altitudes. The local population has always treated us with the utmost kindness and courtesy.

There is much wine produced in the area, but at lower altitudes to our own. Round Puivert the main crops are maize – for cattle food – and sunflowers for the oil found in the seeds. The sunflowers in particular are a stunning sight when in the bloom of their youth, but the crop which is most noticeable to the sense of smell is the humble grass. In warm weather a strong aroma of silage hits a pedestrian when out and about. Something you wouldn't notice while in a car. I think it is called haylage – what you get with those huge rolled up whirls of hay which are then enclosed in plastic. I saw a machine doing the wrapping one day, it's absolutely magic. Something like one of those jugglers who lie on the floor, lift a colleague on to their feet and whirl them round and round.

The haylage sits in the sun stewing away inside the plastic. Even though it is completely wrapped you get this very strong very sweet smell of the fermentation that's going on inside there. Animals, with their sense of smell, must whiff it from much further away. So when the farmers unwrap it for use in winter or in times of drought the critters must go absolutely berserk at this stuff. They probably salivate all summer at the prospect.

And fermentation produces alcohol, does it not? Is it a myth about mad cow disease, then? After all, another name for it is the staggers. Maybe they are just drunk, or, as a good friend of mine would say, "gassed as a carrot". I once read that something like 60% of the road accidents in Sweden are caused by drunken elk, which have picked up fallen fruit, which has then fermented inside them.

Fortunately we don't have too many elk in the area. The big beasts we frequently see are deer and sangliers, or wild boar, both of which are in pestilential numbers. There are 5 million sangliers in France. The French are keen hunters but the sangliers have the upper hand, reproducing faster than they can be killed.

Chapter 5

Day 5. Lavaur to Salvagnac. More background. Protection from dogs. Dr Barbara Moore.

Gay drives me back to the fiveways junction and I once again come through St Pierre, past the old water mill on my way further north.

Every night we have a planning session. Gay can read the maps, physically, which I can't. In fact she is good at map reading anyway. But she can see the tracks on the maps, which I can't. We transfer the information I need into some brief notes of the "turn left, turn right" variety, and I also prod the route into my Satmap Active 10 device.

In the first four days I have walked 139 kms, which is an average of 34.75 per day. Rather more than the 30 kms average I set myself. So how do I feel? At the end of each day my legs are a bit tired and I am beginning to struggle a bit, but by the following morning I am fine. However, my left foot is still a cause for concern.

I am not clear the shoes are the problem. As I said, my feet are very familiar with this type of shoe. On the other hand I have never given them this sort of hammering. On my left foot the big toenail is black and it is going to come off eventually. I damaged that a few weeks ago. This was a self-infliction. I damaged the top of the arch of my foot because of lacing up too tightly. Then I spent some time wearing my shoes very loose in order to ease pressure on the arch. As a result of this looseness my toes were slamming into the front of the shoes and I ended up with a swollen big toe and a bruised toenail.

Also, since I started VBW, I have vandalised the nail on the middle toe of my left foot, the one I have had previous trouble with as a runner. I damaged the nails, then foolishly, to try to give my toes a bit more play in my shoe, I cut the nails back a bit too severely, which has made them worse. They will eventually come off. It's some time since I lost a nail but I seem to remember that it takes weeks or months and it doesn't come off until the one underneath has grown. The real problem comes when it reaches the point where the new one is pushing off the old one and it is more or less detached but not quite so. It is lashing around, lacerating the other toes in the vicinity. I think I need to see a chiropodist and for the duration of this walk at least, have my nails cut professionally to avoid any other problems.

I have seen lots of wild flowers every day. I don't know most of them but I am very pleased to see that the poppies are coming out. One sees a great many poppies in France, in the hedgerows, in the fields amongst the crops. They are just ripening now. There are lots of yellow flowers, purple, white, pink ones, big daisies. It's a pity that I don't know their names. As she is in the same area Gay will see them as well and she will be in raptures.

I cross the river Tarn as I pull into Lisle-sur-Tarn. Some splendid constructions on the river bank, sort of terraces but supported by multiple arches at several levels. This is as far as Gay and I got when we were sussing out the route. So until here this is not entirely unknown territory, but after here it really is terre inconnu.

I pass a huge sign in town for Les Compagnons de Tour de France. Metiers passion d'avenir 22-23 Mai. What's that all about?

A peaceful looking town, but as I pass a house I notice the owners have pinned up a cutting from a newspaper, which says Vandalism in Lisle – in one night the tyres of 20 cars were slashed. Amazing – vandalism is not something we see a lot of in rural France.

I stop for a coffee in Lisle. Lots of half-timbered buildings. Some of these, and other buildings, seem to be made of what I think of as Roman bricks, very shallow bricks.

I use a café where Gay and I had a drink on our reconnaissance trip. The establishment has signs indicating that it specialises in live music. Gay texts me to say she has checked into a campsite at Salvagnac, which is very rural, no electricity, but no fees either. I also receive a text from brother Septimus – who is on a walking cruise (work that one out) in Norway.

The distance markers between Lisle and Salvagnac are very erratic. One in Lisle says Salvagnac 13. A few hundred metres later it says Salvagnac 11. Across the main road and on a bit, a new sign still says 11. I walk another 4 kms – a sign points back to Lisle 3, points on to Salvagnac, 9.

A few kms down this road I pass a very peculiar looking building. Like a mushroom. Don't know whether it is dwelling or industrial or agricultural. We are familiar with a small development of mushroom-shaped houses in Hokitika, New Zealand. Apparently there was a craze for such things in the 60s. Amazingly, if you Google "Dome Homes" you get 281,000 hits. Somebody must love them.

The start of today's walk was very hilly, twisty roads. Then a bit in the middle where it was flat and straight, a Roman road, bringing the bricks? From Lisle to Salvagnac it has become very hilly again.

Only the occasional car passing. I have great views over the rolling countryside. I fall to musing that, apart from the tiredness in my legs – after all I have already walked 30 kms today and 170 in five days – apart from that, this is all very enjoyable.

Although it is hard work, I am achieving something in terms of personal challenge –"the incredible challenge of Vic Heaney", as it says in one of our local French newspapers – and also, by raising funds for such a worthwhile cause, and hopefully raising awareness of what a dreadful illness pancreatic cancer is, that there is no effective treatment, that only research can produce answers, and that money is needed for that research.

I spot a church spire in the distance. This could be my goal, Salvagnac Then I see a very welcome sign as I reach the city limits – a sign saying "pizza au feu du bois".

Our journey from here on will be even more rural, passing through only small villages. I thought I had left the prospect of pizzas behind me for a few weeks. I do like a good pizza, especially from a wood-fired stove, so we shall be off to that restaurant tonight. By a strange coincidence, tomorrow we shall be in Penne – that is the name of tomorrow night's stop, but all Italophiles know that it is also the name of one type of that other traditional Italian dish, pasta.

Gay meets me in the town centre to whisk me off to the campsite she has discovered.

Today's walk was a little shorter, at 31.5 kms. That's 170.5 kms for VBW so far, in total.

Again, most of it was quite hilly, with a total of 837 metres climbed today. I think the climb was even more yesterday but did not make a note of it.

I have now finished the road section of the walk. From here on it will be mostly Grandes Randonnées, or walking tracks. These tend to wander about all over the place, sometimes with big loops of, for instance, 10 kms, which only advance you 2 kms on your way. Where this happens, wherever possible, I will use roads as shortcuts to intersect the loops.

We are camped at Salvagnac, 14, 13, or 11 kms, depending upon which signposts you read, from Lisle sur Tarn.

I have no broadband dongle signal here, although we manage to make a telephone call quite successfully to tomorrow night's campsite at Penne. We are very near a visitor centre. Gay pops across, finds out that they have WiFi and that I am welcome to take my laptop across and communicate with the world. Also, she has bumped into a journalist, who will be visiting us later.

M. Raymond, the journalist, ex-navy and ex-space industry, now retired, comes to pick us up at 6.30 pm, takes some photographs of Gay and myself next to VFO and then drives us into town for a drink so that he can interview us about the walk. The bar turns out to be the same establishment as the pizzeria we have our minds set on. He tells us a few interesting things about the town. It was severely involved in the religious wars with the Huguenots and it was completely "destructed", razed to the ground by the Huguenot forces as was another town nearby in the same year. We have a very pleasant chat and a drink together. Then he takes himself home, where his épouse is awaiting. Gay and I go inside and order pizzas. We ask if we can have some frites for starters. The chips arrive with the pizza but they are most excellent – probably the best chips in France. They are hand carved and nicely browned, they are beautiful. The pizza is good and when the man asks if we want a sweet, Gay says only if you have a crème brulee, because she knows my predilection for this wonderful concoction, which I have discovered only in recent years. He says of course and the crème brulée is excellent as well. Chips, pizza and crème brulée, a quarte of wine and some water – what more could we ask for?

We then walk back to the campsite. This little stroll is actually for me the beginning of tomorrow's walk because the centre of town was the place where I finished yesterday and would have had to start again tomorrow.

—

I mentioned earlier that there are many wild animals in France, some of them large, millions of wild boar, hundreds of thousands of deer, even isolated pockets of bears and wolves. But it isn't the wild animals which are the most dangerous for a walker. As I re-read several books about long distance walks, I kept noting that dogs are a big problem for walkers, especially in France. I must admit that I have never really had much trouble with dogs and I do tend to think that they go for people who they can sense are afraid of them. That's not to say that I would not be cautious with a strange dog approaching.

I once had an article published in the magazine which is now called Runner's World. It was about the danger of being attacked by dogs and my basic recommendation was that you should take another dog with you, as a decoy. I don't have a dog now but something I discovered some time ago – I can't remember whether I read this or discovered it myself – is that if dogs are running towards you, barking and snarling as they do, you should pick up a stone, or appear to pick up a stone, if there doesn't happen to be one there. If you do this, dogs turn tail and run yelping as if they have been hit. It has almost always worked for me and I have done it numerous times. Note the "almost always". I certainly wouldn't rely on that trick if a Doberman or Rottweiler or Pit-bull came charging towards me. I don't know what I would do. It didn't escape my notice that my daughters have quite a collection of dogs between them – surely they would be prepared to consider a temporary loan of a sacrificial dog or two? Perhaps not. I resolved to acquire some suitable equipment. A stick? A pepper spray? A tazer?

I eventually settled for a small pepper spray. I tried to find out whether it would be legal to carry a taser. I received conflicting advice from various forums on the Internet. Then we met a man selling buddhas on a market stall at Mirepoix. He said that at one market of his acquaintance, there had been a tazer stall. He described the awesome noise the things made, which would surely give pause to any marauding dog, or other critters, for that matter. A friend acquired one of these devices for me from Andorra. A hand-held device somewhat like one of the early mobile telephones.

When you press the trigger a spark arcs between two points a centimetre or so apart. I must emphasise that this is something completely different to the tasers used by some police forces, which fire a dart which sticks in the skin – the dart is attached to the hand-held device by wires and when the trigger is pulled electricity flows down the wires with dire consequences for the darted one. It would be virtually impossible to touch my device to any moving creature. I was relying on the sound made, as if the atmosphere is being torn apart.

—

Some time ago I bumped into an acquaintance at a café in Limoux. I told him about my planned walk and some of the matters I was having to take into account, including being a vegetarian lost in France. He said, "So you will be just like Dr Barbara Moore?"

I mentioned her earlier. In 1960, the British press carried daily reports about the progress of Dr Barbara Moore, who was walking from Land's End to John o'Groats. For those who do not know, this is from the southern tip of England to the northern end of Scotland. She accomplished this feat in 23 days. The distance is 874 miles. This is still extremely impressive – her daily distance was about twice that which I was planning.

She went on in 1961 to walk across the USA from San Francisco to New York City, a distance of 3,387 miles, which she completed in 85 days.

One of the reasons the press were so interested in her was that she was a vegetarian. In those days vegetarians were even rarer than they are now, and most people believed that it would be impossible to live a normal life, never mind to undertake such a huge task as this, without a regular intake of good red meat. So the idea of this woman charging such a long distance on such a freaky diet really fuelled the public imagination, or at least that of the press. They probably spent every day waiting for her to collapse, needing a meat infusion.

But no, she walked with only nuts, honey, dried fruits and vegetable juice for her fuel. Even more startling were tales which seeped out of her actually being a breatharian. If you look up that word you will find that breatharians claim to do without food entirely and to assimilate what they need from the air. Barbara Moore herself later claimed to have cut out food and to live only on flavoured water. She said she would live to be 150. She did not, partly because she died as a result of a car accident during her travels in America.

She was not the first to walk from John o' Groats to Land's End, or the other way round. But the publicity which followed her turned the walk into a mass participation sport. In 1960, not many months after Dr Moore's effort, the holiday camp entrepreneur Billy Butlin organised a walking race to follow her route.

There were more than 800 entrants, although rather fewer finishers.

There are now at least two organisations catering for those wanting to make the attempt. Thousands have walked this "classic" journey (which is now so common that it has its own acronyms – JOGLE or LEJOG, depending upon the direction), not to mention those who cycle it or use all sorts of other strange forms of locomotion, including skateboards. The walk has even been completed by a naked man.

Chapter 6

Day 6. Salvagnac to Penne. Pancreatic cancer.

I set out at 6.40. This is real country walking now – no more of your poncey roads. This is down tracks which have been ploughed by tractor tyres in wet weather. Underfoot it is still pretty wet – I don't think I am going to end the day with clean shoes.

A footbridge only a few metres from VFO leads me straight to the beginning of the GR du Pays, which I progress up (and up is the operative word). I am heading for a junction with the GR46, which will then put me on the national network of GRs. The final one of those will be the GR36 which will terminate for me at Ouistreham in Normandy, where our ferry to England will be waiting.

The sky is clear and blue. It is going to be a beautiful day later, but at the moment it is bloody freezing and I wonder why I am not wearing gloves.

About 10 kms into the walk I have been skirting an area which is surrounded by deer fencing. There is a terrific commotion – sounds like a hundred dogs – as if they are tearing something or somebody to pieces. Fortunately I have established that all this is happening on the other side of the fence. There are men scurrying about in the bushes as well. I'll never find out what that's about but it is very puzzling. Perhaps it is a training centre for man-eaters, being trained with live prey – live when they start off, that is.

The track has become even steeper, very up and down. This slows me down a lot, and is definitely not good for the knees.

I spy a dramatic sight ahead and it could mean coffee. The town turns out to be Puycelsi, which is a magnificent mediaeval fortified village, high up over the surrounding plain. Very Italian in appearance. There is a hell of a climb up to it. When I get up to the top, the walls are massive and impregnable, almost as if they are still expecting invaders. These 850 metres of ramparts have seen off various invading forces. Puycelsi was besieged several times: in 1211, 1212, 1213, by Simon de Montfort's forces during the Catholic crusade against the Cathars; in 1320, by the Pastoureaux, a fanatical religious group; in 1386, during the Hundred Years War by the sire de Duras, the English and their mercenaries. And in 2010 by Vic Heancy.

Inside the walls I find lovely streets, very narrow until you get into the centre – obviously all part of the defensive design. I make my way to what I think is a café bar, but is clearly a very smart bistro and restaurant and hotel. I order a nice cup of coffee and a croissant. There are other people in the place, eating breakfast, including croissants. The waiter tells me there are no croissants. I bite back the temptation to point at the other tables. Maybe they have carefully calculated the number of croissants they need for their own hotel guests. I fetch a bun from the nearby boulangerie, proselytise a bit about my walk and pancreatic cancer with some of the other breakfast eaters, and set off down the hill again. Another place which is obviously well worth a visit when we are not so pressed. But what a climb for a cup of coffee.

I am in the forest of la Grésigne, the biggest oak forest in France, which surrounds Puycelsi. I find myself from here on in some very hard country, not only up and down, climbing a lot, but lots of uneven stones, many of them loose. Then places where it is clay and wet and churned up. It is very hard work.

After about 18 kms I find myself on a route forestiere. This is one of the tracks used by forestry people. I am going to be using quite a few of these in the weeks ahead, because there are a lot of forests in France. Four times as much of France is under afforestation as was the case at the end of the Second World War.

The forestry track, although still climbing, is at least clear underfoot. It is not loose or uneven stones, which I seem to have been scrambling over for much of the day.

It's very difficult to estimate how long a walk is going to take when I have no idea of the surface. My normal 6 kms an hour has been more than halved by today's conditions. And since estimation is difficult, how do we arrange a rendezvous time for days when the campsite is not at the end of the walk and Gay is coming to meet me?

A disadvantage of forestry tracks is now signalled by the noise I can hear ahead. The sound of powerful chain saws. They are cutting trees on the hillside, not far above the track. I sound the alarm which is built into my taser so that I can draw their attention and ask if it is OK to go past. They can not hear me, so I climb over a couple of trees which have already fallen across the path and make my way past with some trepidation in case others come hurtling downhill. I am not trespassing, I point out. I am on GR46 but they are taking no precautions about pedestrians.

It is a hot day and now at 19 kms, I suddenly realise that, apart from the coffee in Puycelsi, I have not had a drink since I set off, even though I have 2 litres of water on my back. This is something I have to guard against. I'm not very good at drinking and over the past couple of years I have been trying to train myself to drink little and often, whether I feel like it or not. There is a great danger of becoming dehydrated. I forgot all about it today. Don't tell Gay.

It is very hot and sticky. I get pretty damp even when walking on a cool day, so am sodden on a day like today. Thank goodness for man-made fibres and "technical" sports clothing. A cotton t-shirt, wet through for most of the day, would be tearing my skin off. I mentioned earlier that the only items of my clothing not supplied by Columbia are my socks and underpants. This reminded me of an e-mail sent to us by our NZ friends Robyn and John Davies while they were on a trip to USA. They wondered if I had fully considered the matter of underpants while planning my kit for the walk.

"We met 2 young guys doing the Pacific Crest Trail - Mexico/Canada. They had been going for over 2 months. They had allowed for shoes and sox but never realised they would wear out 4 pairs of shorts and underpants in that time - crutch, and where pack moved on the small of the back! "

That was stunning! I hadn't thought of that one. I have a feeling this e-mail – The Underpants Email – it has such a ring to it – could go down in history with the Zinoviev Letter or the Epistles of the Apostles.

However, I am convinced that my sturdy French underpants will be up to the challenge. And, although the memory is dim, I am sure that students have far more going on in their underpants than a 70 year old man.

I have amazing views of the Gorges of Aveyron as I come down a very long descent out of the forest, on a very loose scree. Very difficult and slow walking. A party passes me toiling up. They are the only other walkers I have seen today and one of the women says to me, "It's better coming down than going up, isn't it?" "No," says I, "it's harder coming down." Certainly for me, on this loose and uneven stuff, with my eye problem.

This has been a very long day, I have been walking for nearly 9 hours, because it has been a bit further than I expected, and because of the terrain, which has slowed me down to half speed or less. About 2 kms from the finish, relaxing because the end is nearby, concerned because I know Gay has made lunch hours earlier and must be worried about me, I find a fence across the path – the GR46, one of France's major pedestrian highways – saying "Closed. Please refer to … (the card is curled up)." Curling is obviously in vogue so I curl my lip and climb over. What am I supposed to do? Go back? To please some bloody-minded farmer? No way! I climb over this fence and another one a few hundred metres further on.

The last kilometre is a descent down very steep rock, I need hands as well as feet, and, being tired, it feels quite dangerous. And interminable. When I get down to the road, the first thing which catches my eye is a wonderful field full of poppies. There must be thousands of them. And there, at the bridge where I arranged to meet Gay, she is waiting. But not alone. Walking towards me over the bridge, carrying the Vic's Big Walk banner, are Ang and Paul, our friends and next-door neighbours. Gay, concerned about my feet, has arranged for them to retrieve the part-worn shoes I donated to another friend, Colin, and to bring them up to relieve my battered end-of-leg things. It must have been an even longer day than I thought when I left "home" this morning there had been no suggestion that they would visit us. In the meantime, they had driven all that way, had lunch with Gay, and accompanied her during the long wait to discover what had become of me.

I had started walking at 6.40 and finish at 16.00, having walked for over 38 kms. I hadn't intended to walk so far – that's a long story, partly about poor estimation. But even if I had, I would have thought maybe six and a half hours, not over nine hours, as it turned out.

The terrain was dreadful for walking. It was it all up and down, even more than the previous days – not only did I walk almost a full marathon today, but I also climbed a total of 1905 metres, which is one and a half times the height of Ben Nevis, Britain's highest mountain.

I gratefully accept a cup of tea and some food. Ang and Paul have had a good look at Penne, about which they rhapsodise. Gay has not because she has loyally stayed at the finishing post, not knowing how delayed I was going to be. Penne is clearly another place we shall have to return to in more leisurely times.

After Ang and Paul have departed, Gay drives us to the campsite which she booked when we were in Salvagnac. We understood it to be in Penne, but it is actually several kms away. It is basically a farm, run by an old couple in their 80s. Or rather by the woman, the man is sitting under a crusader tent. It turns out he has suffered an aneurism. He used to be on the maintenance teams for the platanes. He also used to run the campsite but now he is unable to do so and the old lady does it. It takes us about half an hour to get an electricity hook-up, with various efforts of connecting this wire to that, doesn't work, let's try this one then, et cetera. Very Heath Robinson. We are the only visitors on the campsite and V-Force One is parked in an orchard in all its solitary splendour. Facilities are fairly basic, but they are there and they are all ours. We have a very quiet night.

So what is all this proselytising I do at any opportunity when I meet people? It is about the fundraising. I had hesitated to use the walk as an opportunity to raise funds for a charity. Big televised mass participation events such as the London marathon have become associated in the public mind with fundraising. When we were in the habit of racing every week we would frequently be asked if we were doing it for charity. By the same people who would have been horrified if we asked them every week for a donation.

Raising funds for charities in this way is a great thing, millions of pounds are raised, but so much of it goes on that it is difficult to avoid being asked very often to sponsor somebody, even to sponsor several people in the same event. You have to pick and choose, which means of course you have to say no to some or many, which is embarrassing.

I find it embarrassing to be asked, never mind to do the asking myself. However, many people asked via my blog, on various Internet forums and in person, if I was going to raise funds in this way. Eventually, I decided to do so because it became blindingly obvious to me that there was a cause which was not only deserving, but which had a very personal resonance within my own family. It was something very close to the hearts of Karen and Nicola and me.

Their mother, Gaile, was my first wife. I had known her since she was 14 and I was 15. We married very young and were divorced when I was about 30. She and my daughters moved back to Blackpool, when Karen was 7 and Nicola 3, while I lived in Cheshire. Despite this, I was in regular touch and saw her often because I regularly spent time with the two girls.

When Gaile was diagnosed with pancreatic cancer at the age of 52, I was the first person she asked for and I spent much of the next few weeks sitting by her bedside until she sadly succumbed.

This is how I became aware of what a terrible illness this is. Once diagnosed, there is almost no chance of survival. Pancreatic cancer is savage, vicious, painful and quick. Gaile survived for about 5 weeks. This is normal.

I understand that in a very few cases it is possible to excise a portion of the pancreas and the patient may survive with what is left. I stress that these cases are rare and that by the time of diagnosis, in almost all cases, the cancer has moved beyond that point and the end is both inevitable and in sight.

There is no effective cure for this scourge and no progress has been made in the past 40 or 50 years. Progress will only come through research and clearly research costs money. I understand that although pancreatic cancer accounts for about 5 per cent of cancer deaths, research seeking a cure receives about 1 per cent of cancer research funding.

Pancreatic Cancer UK is a charity started by Sue Ballard. Sue's own husband died from this illness. The aims of Pancreatic Cancer UK are to strive for a good and long life for everyone diagnosed with pancreatic cancer. They work with specialists, research scientists, GPs, patients and their families both nationally and internationally to achieve this.

In the words of the PCUK website:

"We aim to give patients and their families access to the best possible support, information, treatment and care. Through the fundraising activities and donations of our supporters, we fund research into pancreatic cancer, particularly to improve early diagnosis and treatments.

We are committed to raising awareness of pancreatic cancer, providing a powerful voice for everyone who has been affected by the disease."

Once I knew that Pancreatic Cancer UK existed, it was important to me and my family that I should do what I could to help.

Vic's Big Walk became Vic's Big Walk for Pancreatic Cancer UK.

I could raise funds by asking anybody interested or impressed by my walk if they would donate a little to this cause. If I could walk almost 2,000 kms, could they propel some coins or notes in my direction? Or send a few groats electronically to the JustGiving webpage I set up in the name and memory of Gaile? No donation would be too small. I set a target of £7,000. I would have preferred this to be £70,000 in keeping with the 70 years, 70 days theme of the walk, but realistically it seemed to be unattainable. £7,000 would not be much against the millions required, but it all counts. As the Scots expression goes Many a mickle maks a muckle – many small amounts make a large amount.

Hence the proselytising. Whenever I encounter anybody who seems to want to talk, or who says something like "You look as if you mean business" or "You look equipped for anything" or "You walk very fast", I launch into "I have walked here from the Pyrenees". That is guaranteed to start a conversation, during which of course I tell them that I am walking to raise funds for this most worthy of causes.

The address of my JustGiving web page is:
http://www.justgiving.com/Vic-Heaney

Chapter 7

Day 7. Penne to Caylus. Trees.

On Friday morning, after such a long day walking on Thursday, I set off, feeling surprisingly spry, for the next stop. Theoretically, this walk should be under 30 kms. We shall see.

After the first couple of kms, walking along a quiet road, then a track, both low down in the Aveyron Gorge, I cross the road and the track starts to climb in a zigzag, which is always a bit of a pain because for half the time I am walking away from the objective. The track soon turns into the knobbly stone of yesterday. My heart sinks. Fortunately, no loose stone, which would be even worse, especially on the descent. The track flattens out at about 340 metres altitude – I had started at about 100 – and becomes much less stony and much more walkable. I am able to set a reasonable pace.

Soon I realise that I am already some distance off course. I have completely missed the short cut which Gay found for me. My mind has switched onto automatic pilot and I have followed the clearly marked (by a bright purple line) GR46 on my Satmap device. Gay pointed out to me before I started that at one point there is a track which cuts off a big loop in the GR. This short cut stared me in the face, straight ahead, and the GR involved a hairpin bend which took me back south, but still I did not see the obvious.

Later I deliberately ignore the GR where it is clearly going to wander about and give steep climbs over stony hills. If I can see that the road is a more direct alternative – but only if it is safe – I take the road. I have learned something from yesterday's experience. Although most people walking the GRs do so to enjoy the rurality and the challenge of the great rough outdoors, I have a different objective – I need to get North. It is no advantage or pleasure to me, to walk for over 9 hours to cover only 38 kms and to advance, as the crow flies, probably 20 kms in the right direction. From now on, if the road is a better choice to get onwards, and if it is a quiet road, then the road it is for me.

I head towards the wonderfully named Saint-Antonin-Noble-Val. It had been my intention to have coffee there, but instead I stop after 6 kms when I spot a very NZ-looking café by the roadside in the wilds. A very Bohemian, casual looking place. It is just opening for the day. I have to wait for the water to boil. The man tells me he only opens at weekend and he is just limbering up for that. There are lots of tables and chairs on all sorts of rock terraces at different levels on both sides of the road, including down to the river Aveyron. Lovely, scenic place.

Mine host is very friendly. Another man comes in, obviously his copain. We have a bit of a talk about why I am walking. When I come to pay, it is a bit gloomy inside by the till, I have trouble sorting the money out – I don't handle money very often anyway. I eventually let him select the money from my hand. I say I have a problem with my eyes. He says, "Cataracts?" I say, "Yes, but also pattern dystrophy".

"My wife has that," he says. I am not sure by now whether he is talking about the cataracts or the pattern dystrophy. The latter is a fairly rare condition and not to be wished on anybody as it eventually removes the central vision completely. He says, "Vous pouvez voire la femme?" I think, does he mean can I see my wife, but he gestures to something on the wall. When I get close enough I see it is a picture of two women in bikinis. He laughs and says, "See – your eyes are OK really."

Saint-Antonin is another mediaeval town, of which there are so many in France, which has preserved its interior and kept its individuality. Lots of tourists gawping about and parties of schoolchildren having their heritage explained to them.

It is worth recounting this wonderful tale of how Saint-Antonin got its name. It was founded in the 9th century in honour of the saint who brought Christianity to the province of Rouerge, on the western edge of which the town now stands. Successful in this, he decided to convert Pamiers, his hometown in the Pyrenees (Pamiers is 50 kms from Puivert and is where we bought our campervan). But resistance there resulted in his beheading, following which his body was thrown into the Ariège River.

Legend recounts that angels then descended from Heaven to collect the pieces and place them in a boat which, miraculously, floated downstream into the Garonne and on to where the Tarn flows into it; then up the Tarn to its confluence with the Aveyron and up through the Aveyron Gorges to where the Aveyron is approached by the little Bonnette River. There the corpse was retrieved and reassembled by Festus, the Count of Noble-Val, who placed the relics in a reliquary-shrine. The shrine is now lost, which is unfortunate because I am sure today's surgeons would love to study the reassembly techniques.

The sun, which has been so hesitant in arriving this year, seems to have finally made it. The last few days have been cloudless and it is getting to be a bit hot for walking like this, especially as I have not had a chance to acclimatise, it has been so cold. Today is hot, high 20s I would say. Certainly feels like it.

It is in these conditions that a walker really appreciates the Napoleonic trees. It's iconically French, is it not? The long roads lined with platanes, or plane trees. To a motorist they look good, and let him know he is truly in the land of chateaux and champagne. To a hot and bothered hiker, they mean shade and relief from the burning sun. But possibly not for much longer. War has been declared on the trees.

This is because apparently they have the power to attack motorists, causing untold death and destruction.

Front page news in a recent newspaper was that almost a thousand plane trees are being removed, at the rate of 20 a day, on the admittedly dangerous, or at least accident-ridden, road from Carcassonne to Castelnaudary, the home of the Foreign Legion and Cassoulet.

Several other areas local to our home also have planned tree-removal programmes. This is because, according to the newspaper, trees are involved in 7 out of 10 vehicle accidents.

This assault on the platanes has been going on for some time, all over France, and many fear that it will ultimately result in the disappearance of this distinctive feature of the French countryside.

It is said that the trees were planted by Napoleon Bonaparte, or rather at his instigation, to provide shade for his troops as they marched merrily along to invade and subdue all the other countries of Europe. This is very likely a myth as the trees are known to have been prevalent before Napoleon was even a twinkle. Not to mention that, brilliant general though he undoubtedly was, it would have taken extraordinary foresight and planning to have ensured that the trees were up, mature and casting shade in time for his soldiers to benefit. Did he really plan his campaigns 30 or 40 years in advance?

I can confirm that there is a great benefit to the walker from the platanes, especially in the hot months. When I am driving along the same roads, I do not feel threatened by the trees. How can anybody in his right mind think that if a car hits a tree, the tree is to blame?

Of course there are campaigning groups trying to prevent this wholesale destruction of innocent trees. Bodies with names like "Arbres et Routes" and "Amis du Terre" (Friends of the Earth) have had some success in gaining the abandonment of some planned tree removals. Of course these groups claim that the answer should be in changing driver behaviour rather than destroying trees.

But there are other opposing groups, such as one called the Anti-Plane Tree Commando, who one night in recent years sawed down 66 trees on a minor road. The same group, believed to be composed of motorcyclists armed with chain saws, were already believed to be responsible for summarily executing 96 plane trees on another stretch of the same road.

So who will win this battle – the tree huggers or the tree thugs? Well, one thing is for sure – the trees will not be among the winners. And with muddle-headed city hall – the bureaucracy – involved, the odds are definitely on the side of the thugs. In fact, I don't know why the chain saw vigilantes are bothering, when the mairies are doing the job for them. And, as we all know, City Hall never loses.

No, I don't know how long it will take, but it looks like the end of the road for the trees.

From Saint-Antonin to Caylus, where we are staying for the night, I choose the quiet D19, rather than the GR, because it is more direct. Gay sussed out the quietness when she took VFO to the campsite, then reported back via SMS.

I am wearing my older shoes, which were retrieved and brought up by Ang and Paul yesterday. Are they looser? Strange if they are because they are the same type of shoes and same size as those I have been using up to now. Maybe it's psychological; maybe they were made in a different factory; maybe it's the fact that I am not today walking up and especially down – with toes slamming into the front of the shoes – such steep hills. But I decide that they do feel looser, which is good.

I know exactly what speed I walk at on roads, so it is easy for me to give Gay an accurate estimate of when I will arrive. Yesterday she must have waited for over 3 hours. Today I will not be too far out from the estimate.

Here's an interesting story – at least I think it is. When I arrive in Caylus, I can't find the campsite where Gay and V-Force One are already ensconced. She had said in the SMS message that the campsite was really obvious and I couldn't miss it. Later I realise that I must have walked straight past it – you are not as alert when you've walked 30 kms in blazing sunshine. It is lunchtime, so as usual in a French village (another superb mediaeval one) there is nobody to be seen in the streets. I go to a point where I can hear voices from an upstairs window, and I halloo. A voice replies. It takes me a few goes to find which window the head is popping from. I say, "Je cherche le camping." The head says, "Do you speak English?"

The head turns out to be that of Alistair Hamilton, a very Scottish name, but a very Welsh man. In fact a Cardiff supporter. Now the following day, Cardiff are due to play Blackpool at Wembley. The winner will enter the Premiership, which used to be the First Division (this is soccer I am talking about). At least two of my brothers are avid Blackpool supporters. Long ago, Blackpool was one of the top teams and Gaile, my late first wife, in whose memory I am doing this Big Walk to raise funds for Pancreatic Cancer UK, had two uncles playing in the famous "Matthews Cup Final" of 1953, which Blackpool won. In fact one uncle, Harry Johnson, was the captain of the team and the other was Stanley Mortensen, who became in that match the only person ever to score a hat-trick in a Cup Final at Wembley, unlike Stanley Matthews, who didn't score at all. If Blackpool win tomorrow, it will be back to the glory days for them after decades spent in the much lower divisions. At least one of my brothers will be at Wembley tomorrow, and so will all the family of the aforementioned Alistair Hamilton.

So that was enough of a coincidence. But add to that the fact that Alistair and his wife are next week off south to camp in, yes, Puivert, where I live and where I started VBW 7 days ago.

I have walked 33 kms today, which took only 6 hours (a short walk after yesterday) from Penne, and 241 kms for the 7 days.

One thing which is striking me forcibly, especially after I lose it, is the amount of protection, from both wind and cold, afforded by trees.

I am talking here about forests, not the roadside man-hunting trees referred to above. I am being reminded just how much of France is covered in trees. I mentioned that there is now four times as much forest in France as there was at the end of the Second World War. That is very impressive. And much of it is deciduous, although there are plenty of the faster growing conifers, as elsewhere.

I don't know whether I read that figure before or after the big storm of 1999, which felled colossal numbers of trees, as well as doing much other damage, of course.

Read this and weep, those who talk, with that peculiar mixture of horror and pride, about the so-called "hurricane" of 1987 in England.

A few days before the turn of the Millennium (I acknowledge here, before tumbrels of pedantry begin to roll in my direction, that I am talking about the false Millennium which was generally celebrated worldwide on January 1, 2000, rather than the real Millennium a year later), on December 26th 1999, the hurricane Lothar hit France, Switzerland and Germany.

Lothar was the strongest hurricane for 1,000 years. It reached wind speeds of 150 kph in lower areas and 250 kph on some mountains. 92 people were killed in France and power was disrupted to 3,500,000 homes. 60% of roofs in Paris were damaged.

In France a total of 140,000,000 square metres of trees were felled by the storm. I read that the number of trees involved was 29,000,000. Or was it 290,000,000? With numbers like these, does an extra zero matter?

10 years worth of forest production was lost overnight, preventing access by foresters and hunters for months in many areas. Some resort towns did not open for business the following summer.

We experienced some of the aftermath of Lothar. We had heard nothing of it, because we had been in Mexico when it happened. A few months later we were staying at Brantôme, in the Dordogne, a favourite place. We were running in woods with which we were familiar, but which looked strangely different. As if a comet had landed, for instance. There were fallen trees everywhere. The interior landscape of a forest known to us had changed markedly. And it was not just off the beaten track. There was much evidence of tree stumps by the sides of busy roads, giving a faint idea of the number of trees which must have fallen into and across roads. It must have been a terrifying night to be out in a car.

Not to mention that people who had already been primed with dire predictions of what would happen a few days later, as the Millennium arrived, must have really believed that it had all come a few days early.

And their health and tempers would not have been improved much when the storm carried on the next day. Actually, it was another huge storm, name of Martin, which was continuing the work of Lothar. Two for the price of one, and no doubt even more dire tales about it being the beginning of a build-up to Millennium catastrophe.

Chapter 8. The Second Week.

Day 8. Caylus to Concots.

I am five kms out of Caylus, heading North. I am walking past an area on my right, which isn't fenced off, just some grass and then a forest. Signs saying "Domaine Militaire. Defense d'entrer". Just a few yards past one of these signs is a little calvaire, with flowers. Normally if you see that by a roadside you think there has been an accident, but in view of the other sign, I wonder if somebody was shot when they accidentally stepped off the road in the direction of the zone militaire. I learn the lesson.

40 minutes later, I am still going past army bases, truckloads of soldiers going past, groups of soldiers being briefed, signs saying there is shooting 24/7 and don't you dare come near, sounds of shooting, some of it a bit close. But apart from that, I must say that this is a very, very quiet road, traffic-wise, that Gay has picked for me. It's wonderful. I have never seen so many military signs, so many trucks carrying passels of soldier boys. I have never heard so much gunfire since I lived in Stone, near an ammo factory, in the early 60s.

I am always impressed by how tough and fit and smart French soldiers seem. We have a parachute regiment based in Carcassonne and the Foreign Legion at Castelnaudary, so we often have these troops on exercise nearby, or tramping past the house with blackened faces and guns at the ready.

One reason I am walking along this road is because it is straighter than the GR, which swings well away from here. And I may have discovered one of the reasons why. It takes me well over an hour before I am no longer walking past the military signs,

I arrive at Concots. Glory be! Today I had my first walk of under 30 kms – 27 kms in fact – thanks to some nifty work by my navigation officer, and ditching the Grandes Randonnées for the day.

Day 9. Concots to Vers.

I am on the GR36, hardly seen a soul today. All I can hear is bird song, a slight breeze riffling the leaves in the trees. It is fairly easy going, although I have just had a steep climb. The track is heading due north, although I know it is not going to stay that way all day – it is going to double back on itself every now and then, but generally, it is heading north, I am heading where I want to go, moving in the right direction.

When Gay met me in Concots yesterday she said, "What's the matter? You are leaning over sideways really badly." I had been aware for some kilometres that there was a strain on my back and I had thought the constant walking, carrying a rucksack, was having an effect. But it seems that I had developed a severe list to port, what I have seen referred to as "leaning sideways syndrome". I have seen a bit of discussion about this in some of the walking magazines. Nobody seems to be able to explain exactly what causes people to lean over like this after walking for some distance. Apparently it is quite common. Obviously it puts a strain on the back. It's not good. I have to try and guard against that. Apparently we all tend to lean a little, which is why, when blindfolded, we always walk in a circle, and why people get lost in woods when they think they are walking in a straight line.

12 kms into my walk from Concots to Vers, there is an enormous gorge off to my right. Probably the gorge of the River Lot. France is full of gorges and other dramatic scenery.

I hear a man shouting "Heyayayayay!" The forest on my left suddenly opens out into a field. Across the field is a stream of sheep running full pelt at the man who is shouting. He is standing by a water tanker, his hand on the tap, ready to fill the trough from which they will drink. They clearly know what he is there for.

Only a little further down the track I hear some grunting and snorting on my left, which is now forest again. I wonder what we have here. Cows? Boar? Bear? I think we are well away from bear country, which is more or less where I started the walk. A few steps later, I hear some more snorting, then the galloping of hooves, and a herd of wild boar, which are only 10 metres from me, charge away into the forest.

Blackpool did win the big match. I had excited text messages from Karen and Nicola, and my brother Paul. I know my brother Christopher was at the match, so he will be in paradise. I must remind him that a couple of years ago he told me that Blackpool would never make it into the Premiership. Apparently this win is worth £90 million to the club.

We will camp for the night at Vers, pronounced to rhyme with bears. Strangely, one kilometre before Vers is a village called Béars, which is not pronounced to rhyme with bears. Our original estimation of the distance from Concots was 30 kms, but after Gay finished sorting out shortcuts – using the new policy of ignoring the GRs if they wander about too much, it had been whittled down to 22. I pause in Vers, where Gay has booked into a very pleasant campsite next to the River Lot. We meet by arrangement at La Truite d'Orée – the Golden Trout – in Vers, for a coffee, before I walk on to Marty (Jeez! Frasier!). I leave the rucksack with Gay, which really puts a spring in my step. Unfortunately, I also leave the bottle of water she has just bought me to carry the last 5 kms. Some people are just born to be plonkers.

The reason for walking past Vers, even though we are camping there, is to make the 22 kms up to 27, to take a chunk out of tomorrow's planned route, which would otherwise be well over 30.

On the track from Vers to Marty, which is quite narrow, it is fortunate that I am not iPodding or anything else which consumes the ears, so I hear the mountain bike before it comes hurtling past from behind. What happened to the rule that there had to be a bell on a bike, or other audible warning of approach? I think it's great that people can get on mountain bikes and see more of the countryside and enjoy themselves – I do it myself. But without a bell, why do most of these people not have the sense to warn a pedestrian in front of them on a narrow track. That pedestrian could stumble or slip, fall, step sideways, just as the bike is going past. Daft I call it, as Our Ernie's father used to say, every day, in the eponymous cartoon.

And as for the pair who came towards me on ATBs, side by side, not giving an inch, so that I have to step off the track, what a couple of arrogant bastards they are. And I have to say that the majority of mountain bikers, in my experience, in several different countries, behave like this. So do road cyclists – they don't help their own cause – it's no wonder motorists hate them.

So my walk today was 27 kms, the same as yesterday. But what a difference. Yesterday, the shortest walk so far, was also the most tiring, possibly a delayed reaction to the very hard day on Thursday. Today's walk felt like a stroll in the park, and put me up to 295 kms for VBW so far.

The campsite is alongside the river Lot and boats pull in, moor, and can use the facilities. I assume they pay for this, as we do. I talk to a man who comes off one of these boats. He is Israeli. He asks if we have been to St Cirq Lapopie, nearby. We haven't been there, but I have always been attracted by the name. Gay tells me it is supposed to be one of the most beautiful towns in France and the Israeli confirms this. We must go there. He tells me that Israelis love the rivers in France because, apart from the Jordan river, there are no others in Israel. He also says they love to travel because, being surrounded by enemy Arabs, they can not even drive anywhere.

Day 10. Vers to Labastide-Murat.

I have a bit of a problem with my navigation this morning. Gay drives me from Vers to Marty, where I finished yesterday, and I set off. Then I notice my navigation device is on strike. I am entirely dependent on the Satmap Active 10. Gay works out the course on maps, then I feed it into the Active 10.

All I have to do then is follow the course as it appears on the device. Well, the course was in there when I start off, but the other ingredient for successful navigation is missing. We are so deep in the gorge of the River Lot, with huge battlement-like cliffs on either side, that the device can not "acquire" enough satellites to give me a fix.

So I know where I should be but don't know where I am. In fact I am to walk for over 8 kms before the device suddenly locks on and knows where we are.

So I follow the trail for a bit and come to a place where it splits There are two options. One is to go to the right, off and up a narrower track, climbing, the other is straight ahead, flat, and the sign says it is the equestrian option. Both tracks would lead to Labastide-Murat and the difference in the distance is 0.1 kms. So I c–hoose the flat option – who wouldn't? I follow that, and a couple of bends later, I meet the main road and have no idea where to go. So I follow the road signs to Labastide-Murat, still checking on my Satmap to see, by dead reckoning, where I am, because the maps are still in there, of course – it is just the facility which should tell me exactly where I am on the map which is missing.

I head to a point where I can see that the road I am on is not too far from the purple GR that I should be walking on. At that point, I go over a bridge to join my original route and that is where I acquire the signal which gives me an accurate position. This is at 8.8 kms from the start point and comes just as the gorge opens out

I stay with the planned route after that. The strange thing is, when I was walking along the road in a state of bewilderment, not knowing where I was, Gay passed me and didn't stop, smile, wave, or even ask me what the bloody hell I thought I was doing. I wondered if she saw me. I ask her later and she says that, as I had the maps with me (and a magnifying glass) for ultimate backup, she couldn't remember whether I should have been on the road at that point and in any event she had said "Looking good!"

After seeing Gay and before getting a signal, I noticed a hot-air balloon up ahead. Later Gay tells me that she had watched it take off and she had taken some photographs.

I stop off for a coffee in Labastide-Murat after about 24 kms and hear English voices so I lash a couple of VBW cards out. There is a young family just loading their vehicle. Presumably they have been staying at the hotel. They show some interest. They wish me luck with the walk and happy birthday in 60 days. Another English couple have arrived and obviously wonder what this is about so I give them a card and have a bit of a chat. They kindly gave me 5 Euros for the fund, which I later put in the purple collecting tin. They tell me that in Montfaucon, my next stop, there is an excellent orthopaedic hospital, a good restaurant, and a large geriatric home. I'm not sure which of these they are recommending to me.

I meet Gay in Montfaucon, by prior arrangement. The plan is that I could finish there or, if I feel OK at this point, I can walk further to take a bite out of the next day's big walk.

We have a coffee and I walk on. I find myself walking alongside the A20, which feels a bit strange. We have often driven up this road while it was being converted from the RN20 into a motorway. I think it comes up all the way from Toulouse, or even further south. When it first became an autoroute there seemed to be a buzzard sitting on every fence post, with the delight of all the new roadkill that had suddenly appeared for them. And here I am walking alongside it. I remember that it feels a long way from home even when we are driving at this point, so this makes me feel I am getting somewhere.

Gay picks me up and we return to Labastide-Murat, to a fairly primitive municipal campsite. We even walk into town for a drink in the evening, to the same hotel where I received the donation. Labastide-Murat, formerly Labastide-Fortunière was renamed after Napoleon's famed Marshal of France Joachim Murat, who was born there.

Today's walk was 33.5 kms, which means that I have walked 328 kms so far, in the first ten days of VBW.

Day 11. Labastide-Murat to Souillac.

It is an early start from La Bastide Murat this morning. Partly because the forecast is for 31 degrees, the same as yesterday. That is far too hot for this type of activity.

Another reason for the early start is that we tend to wake up as the light filters into V-Force One, and the birds start to sing. That is normally just after five at this time of the year. So I am usually walking well before 7. Yesterday, however, I awoke to hear a bird ringing dem bells, and my mind decided it was time to rise. It took me some time to realise the bird was a nightingale, and that the time was only 2 a.m. Because I had switched into getting-up mode, I slept only fitfully after that. And one does need a good night's sleep every night when walking over 30 kms a day.

I have walked over 10 kms this morning and I have seen one car. Most of my route so far today has been on surfaced roads. The GRs use quite a lot of surfaced roads for some of their length. I think the definition of a GR is that it has to be at least 85% traffic-free.

However, I am not on a GR at the moment. I am on an alternative which Gay has kindly picked out for me. All I can hear is cuckoos, as usual, and other birds from time to time. There is rustle of something in the dry leaves. A snake? A lizard? It is very, very peaceful, with no sounds of man, apart from the rhythmic crunch of my own shoes on tarmac.

The forecast heat is not something to look forward to. It is already quite warm and it is only 8.50 in the morning.

Tomorrow it is forecast to thunder and lightning, which is also not something to look forward to. I'll walk in any weather but I am not happy being out and about, especially on high ground, when lightning bolts are being hurled. From Thursday on it is forecast to be a bit cooler for the rest of the week. Low to mid 20s. I hope that turns out to be true.

I have just seen a sign for a fortified mill, which is an interesting concept. Mills were so important to the life of a community I'm not surprised they would fortify them, but it's the first time I have heard of it.

I stop in Cales for a coffee. It is, as Gay predicted, 17 kms from my start point. She measures this just by looking at the map. We have an electronic thing with a wheel which is supposed to accurately measure distances on the map, but using it hasn't proved to be too successful. Much better to use Gay's eye. In Cales there are two hotels with tables and chairs outside but not a soul at either of them, except myself.

I get to Souillac, a town with which we are familiar, where Gay has set up camp in a very big municipal site. I have walked 31.5 fairly uneventful kilometres today and 359.5 kms in VBW so far.

Day 12. Souillac to Sarlat-le-Canada.

I set off at 6.30. Last night, just after we went to bed, the mother of all thunderstorms arrived. There was a colossal amount of rain. I'm sure it wasn't coming down in drops, just being poured from that huge bucket in the sky

It was like sitting in a carwash for hours, with massive sound effects, as if somebody was playing Gotterdammerung or something on the stereo at the same time as all that water was being thrown at us and the brushes battering the outside of the van, complete with a big flashing light show as well. In its own way, it was magnificent. We were glad not to be in a tent.

The campsite is right by the Dordogne River which is yet another big one. There are so many big rivers in France. This is the one that gives its name to the Dordogne department, which is known to some people as Dordogneshire, in the same way that Tuscany is known as Chiantishire – because so many English people live here.

I head along the river. I am going to be heading almost due west today, to Sarlat. I will make no northerly progress at all. There are rugby pitches on my right, the river on my left, with what looks like a jungle on the other side, a big forest with steam rising – last night's rainfall already being returned to the sky. Very atmospheric.

Very sandy soil here, which is why we were so surprised when we stepped out of VFO this morning, not to find ourselves wading through a sea of mud, despite the colossal amounts of water which fell from the sky last night.

Lots of different cloud formations in the sky, some looking very dark grey. There are more storms forecast for today. I hope I'm not caught out in anything like last night's weather. It's very humid as a result of last night's storm. At first I was thinking I am more tired this morning than I have been, then I realised it is the humidity which is affecting me. It is only seven in the morning but already the heat is dragging the moisture out of the soil.

I am quickly out of town and into farming country again. It's flat at the moment.

I'm sure it's not going to stay that way. The wet grass is lashing against my legs. This is not altogether unpleasant.

I have been walking through a lovely deciduous forest for some kms when I come across a boundary sign. It is the border between the province of Perigord and the province of Quercy, which I am leaving. Between the region of Midi-Pyrenees and Aquitaine, also between départements Lot and Dordogne. All within Occitanie – the Pays d'Oc. This is quite significant for me because I started off in Languedoc Roussillon region, département of Aude, where we live. Within a few kms I was in Midi-Pyrenees, Ariège département. Apart from nosing briefly back into LR on the second day, I have been in MP ever since. And now I have left it. MP is a huge region.

The sign tells a bit of a story historically. The old provinces are from way back. The départements I think were introduced in 1790, following the revolution and with the intention of breaking up old loyalties. The regions in their current form and significance are a recent innovation, brought in by President Miterrand, France's most recent monarch.

And of course Aquitaine is famous in many ways, not least for being the fief of Eleanor of Aquitaine, who was by turns the queen of France and England. She was the wife of Henry the Second of England and the mother of Richard the Lionheart and Bad King John, who did at least live in England, unlike Richard, who visited twice.

I stop for coffee in Carlux. As I am leaving there is a pond on my right. There is a hell of a racket coming from it. I have heard this noise several times and I assumed it was some sort of duck with which I am unfamiliar. But I can see no ducks. I suddenly realise it is frogs. I have never heard frogs like this before. They sound enormous although I am later informed that they are not. Opera singers don't have to be big, do they?

I spend much of today walking through forests. I am still in one, 20 kms into the walk when I receive a text message from Gay, asking where I am and saying she has a map and some advice about a shortcut for the last bit of the walk and that she will come to meet me. Which is good. I think of the Marty Robbins song – "My woman, my woman, my wife".

Ever since I had that trouble last week with the shoes, and the bashing of my toenails on the left foot, the toe next to the big toe – is that the first toe? – was really, really swollen and the nail felt loose. I have had it covered with a Compeed plaster, which is a bit like a blister. Wonderful thing. Terrifically adhesive, and with a wonderful protective gel or liquid or whatever it is. But that toe, which was swollen to twice its normal size, is now back to normal and the nail isn't even black so I don't know whether I am going to lose it. I am certainly going to lose the nail on the big toe, which is black and which is also loose because the other one is growing underneath.

I have been walking on the GR6 today, except for a couple of places where I have used the road to take a kink out of the GR. It doesn't seem to be as much used as the other GRs I have been on. I haven't met a single person – not that I met that many on the other GRs but there have been some, the occasional group of happy wanderers. On this one I almost missed a couple of junctions because they were not obvious where the grass was too long and overgrown – it hadn't been trampled much.

Gay sends me a message that she will meet me in Utilarzac . So I start scanning my route ahead on the Satmap device to see how far ahead that is. I whiz past a place called Villarzac and arrive at the final point of the walk in Sarlat, without even seeing a place called Utilarzac. This is when I realise that the poor old eyes have struck again. I was reading Villarzac on the cellphone as Utilarzac!

When I find Gay, who has walked out 6 kms to find me, the GR is, as with most of today, running through a forest. But at this point, the loggers have been in action this morning. The ground, already softened up by the mighty deluge of the night before, is really churned up. As the track is not flat – indeed there are a number of nasty climbs left in it, we are slipping and sliding all over the place. Also, it is that sort of clay, with Evostik mixed in, which keeps getting thicker and thicker on the bottom of the shoes and one keeps getting taller and taller. Gary Glitter clay, we call it, because it reminds us of his ridiculous shoes. It is a mess, and so is our footwear.

Sarlat-le-Canada is famous for its lovely old buildings and for its huge and splendid markets, but in this weather we do not venture forth to take advantage of the town. Because no sooner have we reached the campsite, had a shower and lunch, than the next thunderstorm arrives, to be followed by two more that evening.

Distance covered is 33.5 kms, 393 kms to date. I have also begun to take note of my climbs. Today my total ascent was 1452 metres.

Day 13. Sarlat-le-Canada to Saint-Léon-sur-Vézère

Before I have done three kms – and the first km is downhill into town – I have climbed 440 metres. Getting out of Sarlat is hard.

One km later, a bit of a problem. They are building a bypass. It cost 4 billion Euros. Which is nice – they always let you know in France how the public money is being spent. But my problem is, although I know where my money is going, I have no idea where my road is. It has been completely obliterated. I am in bewilderment mode. So I do a bit of casting about and time-wasting. Eventually I lay my hands on the remains of the missing road.

Another hill to toil up – deep joy. The course I put into Satmap for today told me there were 891 metres of climb in total. I think I have done most of that already, in the first hour.

I have been walking for about five kms when it starts to rain. I am in an area of fields and woods. For a while I manage to escape from most of the rain under the trees. But then it starts to pour more and more heavily and some of the ground becomes more open, so I get out the big Rohan cape, which goes over my rucksack as well as myself. Trouble is, it's a bit warm in there.

After ten kms wearing the cape I cautiously remove it – the rain seems to have stopped for now, although clearly the weather hasn't made its mind up what it is going to do for the rest of the day. I walk on and at 18.5 kms I come to Marquay. Up a big hill, of course. This is today's coffee break.

Well, here's a fine how do you do? I am just leaving Marquay when Gay texts me to say that the river at Sergiac cannot be crossed without swimming, despite the fact that the Grande Randonnée goes straight across it – the purple line I will be following at that point will invite me to do a Reginald Perrin or a John Stonehouse, leave my clothes on the bank and swim off to oblivion. Gay is going to wait in Sergeac, on the south side of the river and pick me up, drive round to the north side and deposit me there. If anybody thinks that is cheating, don't be silly – what would you do? In fact it means that I have to walk a bit further than otherwise because at the other side, Gay can't get very near, so when she drops me I walk down to the river then back again. Probably adds about a kilometre to the day's walk. But what is one actually supposed to do at this point? We are talking a real river here, healthy and flowing well.

In Saint-Léon-sur-Vézère, after cleaning up, eating lunch, blogging and e-mailing, we walk into town and I have a splendid "glace gourmand" – what I would call a flash ice-cream.

Only 30.3 kms walked today. 423 kms so far. And a "mere" 1276 metres climbed.

Day 14. Saint-Léon-sur-Vézère to Milhac-d'Auberoche

Here's a strange thing to see in France. It's a hammam, which is a Turkish bathhouse. Hammam, Spa, and Salon de Thé. It's out in the country, 3 kms after the start of my walk. What's that all about?

After 7 kms I stop for coffee and croissant in the little town of Plazac. Nice little place, like so many.

I have been walking for several kms down one of these really quiet roads. Not a single car using it. Who pays for all this tarmac? Of course I know who pays for it – me, amongst others but what is the economic justification, when it so rarely gets used. All I can hear is the vague rumble of an aircraft.

I walk on only a couple of kms and I am suddenly assaulted by the sound of cicadas or crickets. Not the first time I have heard them since I left Puivert, but why are they there sometimes and not others? Is it when there are more trees? But you never hear them in the forests. A particular type of tree?

It's dry today, so far, and it was a bit cool when I started out. I wore a jacket, although that soon came off when I started up the now traditional steep climbs.

It's 0920 and still fairly cool. I think, and hope, that it isn't going to get too hot today.

I have walked 14 kms and have just seen a sign saying 7 kms to Milhac-d'Auberoche, which is where I am heading. That is where we are camping tonight. That means 21 kms from St Leon to the campsite. We have already arranged that I will walk several kms past there, because we knew it was going to be under 30 kms. I don't think we realised it was going to be so much under.

Gay is doing an excellent job of chopping kms off the walks. What happened is that Gay planned the route along the Grandes Randonnées, after we decided that walking the whole way on roads would be too dangerous. On about 50 maps – because I can't see the tracks – Gay highlighted the tracks with yellow marker, then I ran over the yellow marker with one of those electronic measuring things, trying to chop the walk into chunks of about 30 kms, consistent with also trying to find a campsite somewhere quite near to the end of each stage. I obviously went a bit awry somewhere, because some of my stages are well over 30 kms. So Gay has been chopping them back really well, by using quiet roads to cut across the big loops in the GRs.

The cuckoos are still pounding away. I heard my first cuckoos this year in March, and here we are, almost into June, and they are still cuckooing.

I am about 3 kms from Milhac-d'Auberoche. I am in the middle of a forest. The track I am walking on is not on the map, and the track I should be walking down does not exist on the ground. I will just have to walk down the track I am on, even though it seems to be going in the wrong direction. It presumably goes somewhere. Eventually, it is intersected by a broad forestry track, which also is not on the map. I turn onto that, and eventually it merges with the purple line on my track, representing the GR. There have obviously been some changes made round here.

The sign back there which said 7 kms to Milhac-d'Auberoche was obviously wrong, because I have already walked 9 since then and I have just passed the entrance to the town. And I have come by a more direct route than the road. It's quite often the case that road distance signs are completely wrong, in any country.

I arrive at the farm which is where we are staying, to find V-Force One parked up among some trees, just at the same time as I pass a pond next to the track. This emphasises even more how incredibly noisy these frogs can be. I go to the vehicle. No sign of Gay. I send her a text message. I holler. I hear her reply and she comes trotting through the trees. It appears she has only just arrived. She was talking to monsieur about booking in procedures and at the same time watching monsieur's son land his plane, which is the one I have been watching zooming around.

Monsieur comes up saying, "You walk too quickly", the implication being that I have caught him with my wife.

We have a cup of tea in the vehicle and then I set off for the final 4 kms of today's walk. I pass the hangar with an aircraft inside. A young man is cleaning it. A nice big strip of field, clearly dedicated to this use, nothing else. Obviously not short of a bob or two if they can waste all that land on a hobby. Not to mention the cost of running a plane anyway. Monsieur breeds geese for foie gras.

Gay had done such a good job of ironing out the kinks in GR36 that from St Leon to here was only 23.5 so, after a cup of tea, I walk on another 4 kms to Leygalie, where I will start tomorrow morning. I am showered, dressed, and fed before 1330.

Today's climb is 1472 metres. I have been walking for two weeks and have covered 450 kms. How am I feeling? A bit tired towards the end of each walk (even a "short" one such as today's) but OK an hour or two later and ready by the next morning for another effort. My feet are certainly in better condition than they were a week ago. Amazingly, I have lost little weight, yet we are not eating big meals and have not even had any wine, except for a small amount on the three occasions we have eaten out.

Chapter 9. The Third Week.

Day 15. Milhac-d'Auberoche to Champcevenil.

It is cold as I start out at the beginning of the 3rd week on 29th May 2010. It's below 10 degrees at the moment but the sky is looking good for a fine day coming up. I hope it doesn't get too hot.

It will be a hard day, Gay tells me, especially near the end. I have to cross a lot of contour lines on the map, which means climb, climb, climb.

There are strange deer noises from the woods. Cows are looking at me, as if to say "Aye, aye, here comes another one".

I am disappointed in my first chance at a coffee stop in Blis et Born, after 6 kms. There is a bar, but it is closed. My next chance is at Le Change, which is at 10 kms. There is another chance at 14 kms, then I have had it – even though it is going to be a very hard day there will be nowhere to have a rest in the second half of the walk. I can stop anywhere, of course, but there is not usually anywhere to sit down unless there is a bar. And it's not so much the coffee. Coffee makes me take at least a few minutes, whereas if I sit down for a rest out on the open road I soon get up and get cracking.

I manage coffee and croissant in le Change. A few kms later I am passing a farm settlement. Various dogs come hurtling at me, including one big Alsatian, which looks particularly keen. As it comes in for the kill I fire up the stun gun and give it a few bursts of static. Fortunately the dog is not deaf and it backs off a little.

Where the bloody hell is the track? It has disappeared. It is here on my mapping device, as it was on the paper maps, but I have come to a dead end, with an impenetrable thicket. This is at Gros-Jean, after about 12 kms. I speak to an old man, with two walking sticks. "Le sentier, n'existe plus", he says. The track no longer exists.

Oh great! I zoom out on my Satmap and look for a way round, via various roads, which should connect with the same GR some distance away. It means I have to go back a couple of kms. This is not the first time today that the track on the ground has not matched the one on the map. And it means going back past those dogs. They seem to remember that I have thunder and lightning in my hands and slink away.

A few extra kms added on to what was already going to be a hard day. I have to go back almost into Le Change before starting the detour.

In the well-heeled looking village of Bas Lauterie a man congratulates me on my vigorous walking. He says I am going well. So we have a chat about what I am doing, and I give him one of my cards. And he donates me a leaflet – this is when I realise I am in the hands of the Jehovah's Witnesses. A bit further on I put the leaflet through somebody's letter box and am on my way.

I saw a weather forecast in the paper when I was having coffee. It is going to rain for the next couple of days then it is going to ramp up to 30 degrees again. Both things to look forward to.

The cuckoos are still going on. I don't know if anybody has estimated the numbers of all the cuckoos in France – there must be millions. There seems to be one round every corner. Yet you never see one. We had the good fortune once to see a group of migratory cuckoos when we lived in Cyprus. They are a very hawk-shaped bird, but with a straight beak. We were very puzzled as to what they were but somebody kindly enlightened us.

Another bird I have heard more than once this morning and frequently during the walk is the woodpecker, battering hell out of some trees. I was with my brother CD recently in Stanley Park, Blackpool. There was a woodpecker doing its thing and I remarked on it. I was surprised to find that he didn't know the sound. He must have heard it, but had never associated it with Woody Woodpecker.

I was told by Usas, one of the people who advised me, in the Total France forums, about my course up through France, that the GR36 was like the M1 of footpaths and that it would be impossible to get lost. We have already disproved the bit about getting lost and also, although I have been on the GR36 for 3 days now, I have yet to see another walker.

I made a bit of a navigation error. I was daydreaming and obviously hadn't looked at my Satmap for some time. Found myself well beyond – a couple of kms past – where I should have turned. I can get out of it by using the zooming out technique and looking at where my planned route is, compared with where I am and then follow the logical paths to meet up with the GR further along, but this adds more wasted extra kms. I have missed my turnings before, but normally it has been only a couple of hundred metres past the turn and it has been easy to go back and make the correction, but, as my mother told me more than once, this time I have gone too far.

I have rejoined the track now, at the ends of the earth – a place called le Boute du Monde – which is actually the name of a restaurant we know in Akaroa, New Zealand.

This is another place where the track disappears. Where the track should continue, there is a house. No sign of where the GR should be. At this point the track doubles as both GR36 and GR646, but they have equally disappeared. I backtrack and find a footpath which goes at right angles to the alleged direction of the GRs. It is unmarked so it could be a waste of time and kms trying it. I go down there and eventually I see the red and white GR markers – why was there not one where the footpath met the road, where one is really needed? All these questions and so few answers.

The mapmakers' guild of the Dordogne should be sacked en masse and somebody brought in from headquarters to restore order. I think it is five times on today's walk that I have gone wrong – there were a couple of occasions I haven't troubled you with.

I eventually arrive in Champcevenil. Gay picks me up there and drives us to Brantôme, where we shall stay the next two nights, it being one of our favourite places.

There is still a troglodytic element in much of the Dordogne. In Brantôme, for instance, many of the shops are in caves, with a normal shop front. Many of the people live in caves, with a normal house front. This evening, we hope to dine in a cave, one in which people lived 8,000 years ago. Our pizza will be cooked where those people prepared their own food. How cool is that?

I walked 33.5 kms, giving a VBW total so far of 484. Total ascents today were 1608 metres, which is quite enough.

The navigation officer is in the throes of some drastic rerouting, which will probably mean that we shall not be going through some of the places on the schedule I published some time ago on my blog.

Day 16. Champcevenil to Brantôme.

Sunday morning in Brantôme. It has been chucking it down virtually since we arrived yesterday afternoon. As I leave there is nobody to be seen. Just a moorhen picking her way around the tables of a restaurant where nobody was sitting last night because it was so wet. A heron lumbers overhead as I look from the bridge down to the old water mill – now a superb restaurant – and the abbey. It's going to be a very wet day.

Yesterday, when I met Gay in Champcevenil I had a shower in V-Force One, then we had lunch, all of this in a cemetery car park, before we drove to Brantôme. The plan was that today she would drive me back to Champcevenil and I would walk the rest of the way back to Brantôme, from where I would set off tomorrow morning, heading northwards. But the campsite is under lock and key until 8 am and we couldn't get the vehicle out. So I am actually walking today's stage in reverse, heading back south, in the direction of home, from Brantôme, back to Champcevenil, where Gay will pick me up again later, for another night in Brantôme, where we are going out for dinner tonight.

Brantôme was a great disappointment to us last night. Not only was it wet and horrid – still beautiful, but much less so in the rain – but the pizzeria in the prehistoric cave, which we had been so looking forward to, is closed until 2nd June, so we weren't able to go. Most of the other restaurants seem to serve meals only at lunchtime. We ended up having a very pedestrian (how appropriate) snack in a gash café. But it was in a cave so all was not lost. I had omelette and chips and Gay had a salad.

I also had a crème brulee, which was poor, a bit like semolina in consistency.

Not much else to say about my walk today. It started off wet and miserable, it was wet and miserable at the end, and the bits in between were the same. Not much fun, and not one café or bar in sight the whole way.

When I was a lad, before the invention of rock'n'roll, some of the biggest names in popular records were Frankie Laine, Guy Mitchell, Nat King Cole and Johnny Ray. Frankie Laine had a big hit with "Rain, Rain, Rain" (behold the ark is made), while Johnny Ray used to cry (literally, he was a very emotional man with a hearing aid, collapsible legs and well-supplied tearducts) "Walking In The Rain" (just a-trying to forget).

Well, Johnny, I have been doing quite a lot of walking in the rain lately. And Frankie, if we could only get hold of a joiner in France (just the same as England, it is impossible to get anybody in the building trade) that ark would be taking shape right now.

I walked 27 kms, which brings the total covered so far to 511 kms. And, if I have confused you above, that means we have now officially reached Brantôme. We first discovered this place, many years ago, when driving in a campervan from La Rochelle to Carcassonne. It was mid-afternoon and we were ready for a break. We saw a sign, saying "Brantôme, Venice of the Perigord" so we pulled off into the town for a cuppa. 3 days later we moved on. It is magic. A loop in the river has been cut by a canal, so that the river and canal give the effect of the whole place being on water. There are even gondoliers. All this, many wonderful old buildings and one of the best restaurants – the Moulin d'Abbaye – we have ever come across, make it a very special place for us, and for many others.

Gay has been doing some drastic re-routing, now that I have decided that roads are more to be pitied than scorned, and especially where the GRs diverge wildly from the northerly direction. The first fruits of this new policy come tomorrow, when I shall be walking from Brantôme, not to La-Beaudrigie, as previously announced, but to St Martial-de-Valette.

Day 17. Brantôme to Nontron.

Last night we had our first social engagement of VBW. We were entertained to dinner by Pam and Bob Coxon, who live near Brantôme. It was a good meal and a very enjoyable occasion. We had not met before but Gay and I feel we have made lasting friends. Contact came when Pam donated to Pancreatic Cancer research through my blog, having recently lost her sister to the appalling illness.

The day starts a little better than yesterday. Everywhere is wet but nothing is falling from the sky as I set out from Brantôme, past the guilty pizzeria, and head a bit west but mainly north, on Gay's newly replanned route. The weather soon changes. A light drizzle descends. Then there is a lull for a couple of hours, during which I am even able to remove my waterproof cape

At 11 kms I pass through St-Crepin-de-Richemont – what a wonderful name. In a hamlet called Chancevil, I expect to see a gambling den or two but am severely disappointed.

Another walk with not a coffee shop or bar the whole way. No excuse to sit for a few minutes, with its effect of wonderfully renovating the legs for a while.

The occasional dog comes out to circle round behind me. The occasional taser is cocked and ready, but no actual combat ensues.

As I near the finish the rain starts again, becomes more serious, and settles in for a few hours. I reach the campsite to find that St-Martial is a suburb of Nontron and that we have been to Nontron before. The approach is extremely dismal, but the campsite itself is fine. Gay tells me that the owners are very nice, are much taken with news of my walk, are keen to meet me so they can marvel, and have given us a discount. The discount will go in the purple collection tub for Pancreatic Cancer UK, of course.

The newly-revamped route which Gay has been slaving over proved to be excellent. Very quiet roads running through just a few working hamlets. The only slight snag was that none of the places I passed through was big enough to host a café or a bar. I look forward to these not so much for the coffee as for the rest. I used to charge along for the full walk but have now realised the value of a short rest. A coffee, perchance a croissant, ensures that the break lasts longer than an impatient two minutes.

I covered 26 kms, bringing the total for the 17 days to 537. Total ascents today were 1157 metres.

Day 18. Nontron to Roussines.

A sharp climb out of Nontron first thing.

I'm glad I didn't put a waterproof on, even though it is trying to drizzle. My back is very damp already as a result of these exertions, so it would have been even worse in waterproofs.

Nontron is a town which seems to be very run down in parts. It is centred on the knife industry – those little knives that all Frenchmen wear in holsters on their belts in case they should meet a piece of cheese or need to defend themselves against a sanglier. Like the Laguiole or the Opinel, although the one they make here is the Perigourd de Nontron. There is a big knife fair in Nontron every August.

I assume it used to be a cottage industry, with people making the knives at home, in little workshops in their houses – funnily enough, the three houses next to our own in Puivert used to do the same thing – but now it is all done in a modern factory.

A lot of the houses seem to have workshops attached to them, or below them. Many are sad-looking or derelict.

Gay says we have been here before but I can only vaguely remember it. We went to the knife factory but it was a Sunday or another day of no work, so although we saw displays we didn't get to see any actual knife-making.

Nontron has an interesting history. It was founded by Phoenicians. It was sacked by Saracens in the 7th Century, proving that militant Muslims are not a new thing. Some say that Richard the Lionheart met his end here, but that is generally reckoned to have happened at Châlus. But long before any of that, prehistoric man was putting paintings on the walls of the nearby Cave of Villars, so that we could still be marvelling at them in the age of television and 3-D, computer-animated films.

Before I leave town, I find I am in a completely different type of area – it is looking very swish round here. It's funny how, as I have walked along, I have noticed how regionalised France is in so many ways. For instance, several days have passed since I saw a vineyard. The countryside I have been passing through for the last few days seems to grow mainly wheat and animals. Another thing – the signs for town centres, which in most parts of France would say "Centre ville", have been saying "bourg". Another sign frequently seen in this area is "Parking Chasse", which is something I have never seen before. There is lots of hunting everywhere, but not usually with all this designated parking.

Today's course carries me pretty much due north. The GR 36 would have taken me in a great sweep to the East so I won't be using that for a while. Today I pass out of the Dordogne département into Charente, which also means I leave the region of Aquitaine and enter Poitou-Charente, the fief of Ségolène Royal, who was the defeated candidate of the Left in the last presidential election in France.

I had covered 538 kms as of yesterday, which seems a long way but it is only just over a quarter of my total distance. I am not yet halfway through France. I'm in reasonably good condition. I have lost only a little weight, maybe 2 or 2.5 kilos. My feet are OK, except that of course I am going to lose two nails. The nail on the big toe of my left foot is now looking pretty loose, so I hope the replacement is well on its way underneath. I am suffering a bit from arthritis in the joint of my big toe, again on the left foot. I don't know whether that is encouraged by the damp weather we have been having. It is forecast to return to hot weather tomorrow. Deep joy.

For the past 3 wet days I have not seen a coffee shop or bar during my walks. So imagine my delight when, as I come into the village of St Estèphe (St Steve) I see a sign saying "Café et Brocante. 200 metres". St Steve goes up in my estimation, it will be the scene of me drinking my first coffee for days. The town is the centre of one of the four appellations of the Médoc wine region so of course it is big enough to warrant a café. Or is it? Of course I have to walk much more than 200 metres before I pass a boulangerie, which is closed, then I get to the Café/Brocante, which of course is also closed. I sit opposite, on a school step, using my poncho as a cushion because the step is wet. I eat a sandwich. Eventually a woman comes out of the door of the café. I ask if it will be open today. She says no. I ask if there is another one. She says yes, opposite the cemetery, at the supermarket there is a café.

So I walk on and find that it is one of those arrangements where there is a small "supermarket" with a café by the side of it, both served by the same person. It is shut, nobody there, although the television is on in the café. I hang around for a couple of minutes and a man comes tearing up in a car. I ask if he will be open today. He says of course yes, he has been for the bread. I ask for a coffee and a croissant. He says no croissants, the boulangerie is closed. So where has he been for the bread, and does that not normally include croissants?

He has impossibly white capped teeth. He asks if I am on holiday so I tell him what I am doing. He asks me a few questions about it then he keeps saying, "Bon courage! monsieur. Formidable! Bon chance! Vous etes tres courageux!" He must repeat all this about ten times, including again as a final benedicition as I leave after my coffee.

Some time later I arrive in Busserolles. I ask a woman if there is a café. She says "No thanks, I don't want a coffee." I look puzzled. She says, "Oh, pardon me monsieur, there is a café high up but the square is closed." Que? I walk along and find that the café in the square is closed. I ask somebody where the other café is and they say it is 50 metres round the corner. They don't mention the "up" bit, but I soon find out what the other woman meant. The 50 metres is at least 200 metres and "high up" means there is a decent climb. I find a bar. I go in and there is a man hanging about. He is actually hanging about outside but when he sees me he goes in just in front of me. I gather he is not the proprietor but of the latter there is no sign. Another man comes in and greets the first one. They sit down together. I put my rucksack and hat down on a chair. An old man, must be at least 85, possibly older, comes shuffling out of another part of the establishment, wearing a purple jumper and slippers. He shakes my hand and says, "Ça va?" as if he knows me. Of course I confess that I am fine. He shakes hands with the other fellows and pours them some drinks. Then he asks me what I would like. I tell him and find he is deaf. Eventually I get through to him that I want a grand crème and he shuffles off back where he came from, presumably tells his wife to make a coffee, comes back again. He goes in a cupboard for a cup. He brings me a cup with some coffee in, also a bottle of milk. He has already brought some sugar. I ask if he has a croissant. He goes off and comes back with one of those plastic packets in which supermarkets sell factory-made croissants to the desperate. There is one croissant in there. It is nothing like a real croissant, but I eat it. By this time there are three men, who are on their second drinks. As I leave the old fellow smiles, the old lady beams, the other men are all quite friendly in their goodbyes and I am off.

I am meeting Gay at a crossroads by a calvaire because the campsite is well off the route. She will be bringing me back to the same point in the morning. Otherwise I would waste several kms today and tomorrow.

The weather really becomes serious about raining while I am in the last couple of kms of the walk so I am glad to see VFO and Gay waiting for me at the appointed place.

Vic's Big Walk is long, and a huge undertaking, but I am regarding it as an elephant task. You know what that is? Not many of us could look at an elephant and think, "I'll eat that". But it is possible to say that you will eat a bit of an elephant every day and, over a period of time, consume the whole elephant.

Similarly, a walk of 2,000 kms is a bit daunting, so I regard it as 70 shorter daily walks of about 30 kms. And each daily walk I divide up into three 10 kms walks, hopefully intersected by coffee stops. It's not so much the coffee I want, as its assistance with my elephant task.

Today has been just another miserable trudge through the wet. A day in which I saw few crops (I haven't seen a vineyard for days, despite St Steve's provenance). A day in which I was regarded by insolent cows and ignored by arrogant horses. A day, also, in which I passed from the Dordogne département into Charente, and from the Aquitaine region into Poitou-Charentes. A day in which I inserted the fourth mapping card into my Satmap Active 10 navigation device, which is proving invaluable in keeping me on track.

We are at Roussines. I walked 29.5 kms (don't begrudge me these half kilometres – I have to work for them), and climbed a total of 1343 metres. So far I have walked 566.5 kms and am now past a quarter of the walk, in terms of time.

Day 19. Roussines to St. Maurice-des-Lions.

Off before seven. After our arrival at the campsite yesterday it rained pretty much for the rest of the day. The campsite looked as if it was really nice, if only we had a boat to travel round it. Each vehicle had a large bay. Unfortunately the grass was a bit long so that meant every time we walked through it our shoes became wet. Both my pairs of shoes are now sodden.

Today is supposed to be drier. We'll see. It is also supposed to getting too warm for a walker's comfort. I am passing a lot of what the French call étangs, small lakes. It seems a very nice area, with the lakes and woods. It is still pasture land, lots of cows.

I like it when the track on my navigation device points due north as it has been doing for most of today. I am coming up to a place called Cognac here. Not the well-known one, I think, unless they manage all that brandy production in two houses.

I have cows galloping around in field alongside me. I have had this quite a lot in the last few days. They charge along, stop, stare at me, charge along again, following my course. I am glad there is some fence between them and me. Cows can be very aggressive. Bullfighters use cows for their practice sessions.

I stop in Suris, which is about 16 kms into the walk. See a café, go in. Turns out to be run by some English people. Don't do croissants, so I have coffee and toast. All the signs for food are in English. They say they can't get French people to come in. They come from Hampshire, which I shall be walking through when I debark from the ferry in Portsmouth. The man says what a hard life it is, running the bar. They love being here but they don't make any money and the Government take 60% of their earnings in tax. This is strange because as an individual you pay less tax in France than in UK. He also says that when you first set up in business, the Government assumes a certain level of profit and takes 60% of that in tax, which has to be paid monthly, for three years, and if you are not careful you get stuck with that for ever.

They (the café owners, not the Government) have line-dancing nights. Line dancing, along with country music, is very popular in France. I have learned to play the guitar since I turned 60. My very first performance in public was in December 2008. This was at a line dance demonstration in Lavelanet. Fortunately I was part of a large band with lots of guitars, so there was safety in the numbers. This café in Suris will be having a dance on 23rd July, which is of course my birthday. I tell them I would love to be there but I will be otherwise engaged, hopefully arriving at the destination. Lots of interesting pictures in the bar. The second time in a week that I have seen the famous picture of the skyscraper men sitting on the girder high above NewYork.

Again I meet Gay at a lonely cross-roads and she takes me to St-Maurice-des-Lions, where the campsite is even lonelier. Not for the first time, we are the only occupants. It is a decent size but we are the first customers of the year because they opened only yesterday, 1st June. It is just outside St-Maurice. A very kind gentleman contacted us a few days ago by e-mail and offered us the use of his house, even though he would not yet have arrived here. A wonderfully generous offer, but not one we would have felt comfortable accepting, in his absence.

It has been dry all day, but not too hot yet. I believe that is in the offing.

We are now more or less in the plumb centre of France. Gay has wielded the navigational axe and we are heading more or less due north.

Day 20. St. Maurice-des-Lions to Availles-Limouzine.

It's cold as I set out at 6.30. The sky is clear. Not a cloud. It's going to be a fine day. The birds sound much happier. There are streaks of mist lying through the trees, with the sun shining through the wisps. A good photographer could work wonders with that. Gay has run me back to the place where she picked me up yesterday and I am now walking through St Maurice, looking forward to coffee in Confolens, which is about a third of the way into the walk.

Nicola sent me a text earlier – in fact I think she sent it last night, saying, "Good morning. Happy Day Twenty. Have you heard about the mad gunman in Cumbria yesterday. He killed 12 people and injured 25 around Whitehaven and Gosforth." That's the area my mother hailed from. Nicola also added, "p.s. 75 fans on Facebook now." She and Karen have set up a VBW page on Facebook. Kait from Pancreatic Cancer UK told me in an e-mail yesterday that there is a lot of activity going on about me on Twitter.

It is 4 kms from the start point to St-Maurice, then, at another 6 kms past St-Maurice, which we all know is coffee time, I enter Confolens. A long downhill into this town, which I am pretty sure means a long uphill out the other side.

It's a big town by the standards of those I have been seeing lately. Lots of boulangeries, lots of cafes. I have even just seen a shop that says "Fish and chips". A lot of English people round here, then.

I have coffee and a croissant in a busy bar. Seems like a thriving place, this. Anyway, I eat the croissant, then I notice all the boulangeries nearby. There are three in the same street as the bar. I could have had something a little more tasty.

I remove my jacket while in the bar because it is nice and warm outside now, although the day started off a bit sharp. I also do something very unusual in Confolens, for me. I take some money out of the bank. I very rarely touch money. We are nearly always together, and Gay usually handles the filthy stuff. But on this trip, I am carrying a little for coffees, et cetera, and for emergencies, so rather than keep bothering Gay for pocket money, I actually took some from a hole in the wall, which is revolutionary.

Here comes a big hill. I was right about the big climb out of Confolens. This hill is of Olympic standard, I would say. All that training in the hills of New Zealand pays off when I meet climbs like this.

A couple in a car near the bottom of the hill have to pause at a traffic calmer. The woman does a double-take and really waves at me as if she knows me. Maybe she is just friendly, but there may have been something in the papers. Columbia have been feeding the newspapers by rota as I go up the country and there may be articles appearing without me knowing anything about it.

I am soon out in the country again. Quiet as anything. I could be back in the Middle Ages here. Timeless. Nothing changes. All I can hear is the sound of dogs barking, a woodpecker, a jet plane overhead, the sight of a big telephone tower in the distance, and now there is a truck heading towards me, down a very narrow lane. But seriously, generally all is peace, apart from these slight interruptions

After 18 kms I stop in the beautiful village of St Germain de Confolens. There is a lovely ruined chateau. As I walk down through the town I pass a luthier, which must be a nice job to have. I have a coffee at what looks like a nice restaurant with a balcony overlooking the river and the bridge. It would be grand to sit here at lunchtime and be forced to have that view for a couple of hours. But I settle for a banana with the drink.

Coming out of St Germain I miss the turning onto the GR48. This is mainly because I don't realise that you have to go through a quarry to get to the trail. When I do get onto the track it is really overgrown – I don't think this bit gets used very much at all.

I have seen nothing yet. I don't think anybody has been along here for months, or maybe this year at all. I am pretty sure it is another GR where they have changed the course and we still have the old course on the maps. Now I am wading through waist-high, soaking grass, nettles, bracken and brambles. It isn't much fun. This goes on for several kms. I think I can confirm that it is an obsolete GR.

I am walking alongside the Vienne river. So much for my recently dried-out shoes. The vegetation, despite it being such a sunny day, has not had a chance to dry out. It is wet through, and so am I now.

I arrive in Availles-Limouzine. Today I walked 27 kms, with a total ascent of 1052 metres. I have walked 623 (and a half!) kms since setting out on this venture.

We are camped very pleasantly by the Vienne River.

I have mentioned that I seem not to be losing much weight, but really it is very difficult to say whether I am losing any, or how much I am losing. The situation is clouded by water retention in hot weather and water rejection in cold weather, but it seems now that I am losing about 1 kg per week. That's fine – I had too many anyway.

Day 21. Availles-Limouzine to Persac.

As I start out it is another brilliantly sunny morning. Not a cloud in any direction. Gay has dropped me off at the place where she collected me last night. Very few signs of civilisation. A little burst of traffic sound in the distance, birds singing, the roar of wheat bursting towards the sky.

The campsite which was our base last night was very nice. It was by the Vienne river which, although it is nowhere near the sea at this point is wide and flowing well. Gay went for a little walk on the campsite. There were lots of frogs – again – making their noises and popping in and out of the water. She was watching these, then a duck with a troop of babies, when she saw something else in the water near them. She thought it was some predator going to get the ducklings. It turned out to be a coypu. I don't know whether coypu do grab baby ducks but this one didn't. She watched it for a while and saw it go into its hole in the bank, but she failed to get a decent photograph of it. Shame.

I am on a GR again. In this case it is the most direct route to where I am going.

I think it is the GR48. Really badly eroded. It's probably a torrent when it is raining. There is a huge cleft down the middle, maybe two or three feet deep. It makes it hard work to go along here, going up and down steep hills, almost hands and knees stuff. I think the GR planners are sadists. They deliberately cast aside any options which would involve flatness or smooth ground to walk on. They look for steep up and down, twisting turns and loose stones or big stones which make walking difficult. I much prefer the roads – the quiet roads, that is. Progress is slow in places like this.

Now I am onto farm track again, able to maintain my normal pace, then before you know it I am back on surfaced road. This variety makes it difficult to estimate how long a walk is going to take. It depends on the ratio of road to GR and it depends on the condition of the GR.

Yesterday we passed from the Charente département into Vienne. You can always tell by the change in the car number plates. We are still in the Poitou-Charente region.

After about 10 kms I come into Millac, which I am hoping is where my first coffee stop is. I am swiftly disabused of that idea. I ask a woman who is opening her shutters and she say no, there is no café or bar or boulangerie in Millac.

Gay texts me to say that l'Isle-Jourdain looks a good place for a coffee stop and that it is a nice, tidy town. It's about 5 kms further on, about halfway through the walk.

Having paused in l'Isle-Jourdain to identify the coffee stop for me, Gay drives on to Persac, where she finds that the campsite does not open until June 15th (this gives them a season of two and a half months, which only bureaucrats running a business would find acceptable). She enquired about all this at the Mairie. Also visiting the Mairie was Jacques Felix, who was there for a meeting about his property. He volunteered the use of his orchard and his electricity.

Today's march was 30 kms, bringing the total to 653.5. Total ascents today were 966 metres, under a thousand for the first time in living memory. I started keeping a record of the climbs when it struck me, after all that talk about Ben Nevis, that I am probably climbing Everest every week, as well as walking over 200 kms .Statistics show that this may be correct.

I have been feeling very guilty about this being known as Vic's Big Walk. There is somebody else who is spending at least as much time and effort as I am. Gay is doing everything except the walking.

We get up at about five in the morning. While I go to the facilities and have a shave, et cetera, Gay is making a cup of tea, putting out my breakfast, making me some sandwiches to take with me, getting me out a banana, and putting out a bottle of the beetroot juice to drink before I start the walk.

We have breakfast then I continue to get myself ready. Gay washes the dishes, then she unsecures the umbilical for the vehicle, turns off the gas, demounts the window blinds and generally gets the vehicle ready for moving.

Then she drives me to the point where I finished the previous day's walk. She sees me on my way. Then she does housekeepery things with the vehicle, she goes for fuel if necessary, she goes for food. She is not necessarily going the same route as me and needs to seek out shops, perchance a supermarket.

If she is able to travel roughly the same route that I will be walking she even stops to suss out where there are suitable coffee stops for me, then texts me to let me know where the coffee shop is in relation to the track that I will be walking on.

She then goes to find the next campsite. She checks in at the campsite. After checking in she probably washes some clothes – don't forget I am producing sweaty clothes every day. She then decamps – unless the campsite is on my route and I will walk straight to it – and goes to wait for me at an appointed meeting place. She sometimes sits there for hours waiting for me because it is not always easy to estimate how long a walk will take, particularly if I am going to be on rough and mountainous tracks.

She picks me up, takes me to the campsite. While I am having a shower and getting myself sorted, she makes the lunch. We eat lunch. Then, while I am writing my blog and dealing with e mail correspondence, Gay washes the dishes and other necessary jobs.

She then even attends to my feet and toenails, especially after the trouble I had in the first week. She spends hours every day poring over maps, particularly for days and days at a time when she was re-planning the route because it was clear that I was walking far too long each day on the stages we had selected.

Then we sit down and have a meeting about the next day's walk. She gives me instructions on the route – don't forget I can't see the tracks on the maps – which I then feed into my invaluable Satmap Active 10 navigation device, ready for use the following day. By this time it is getting on for evening meal time. She prepares that, we eat it. Then, while I transcribe the notes which I have dictated in a tape recorder – which I hope will form the basis of a book – she washes the dishes. If we are lucky we then snatch time for a crossword and maybe a few pages of reading. By which time it is bedtime. While I go to the ablution block to get myself ready for bed, Gay closes all the shutters on the windows. We are in bed by nine o'clock because we shall be getting up at five.

So, all day, every day, Gay is going full tilt. She is a treasure. I love her. I couldn't do this walk without her. It is no wonder that so many people say to me, "Vic, you are a very lucky man." And I know it.

Chapter 10. The Fourth Week

Day 22. Persac to St. Savin.

Another Saturday, another week starting.

We had an interesting time with Jacques yesterday. He is French, but has been living in Quebec for most of his life and now has dual French and Canadian citizenship. In fact he is from Persac and spends part of the year there now, every year, in an old house which was one of the family houses. He told Gay we could park in his orchard, next to a cherry tree, which is right up Gay's street. She loves cherries and proceeded to prove it.

He was very talkative and friendly. We would have loved to spend more time with him but we don't have much spare time during this walk. We went to his house after Gay picked me up and I had a shower and we ate lunch at the pickup point. Jacques talked a lot, which is fine, because he was very interesting, but I was itching to be writing my blog. Eventually he said well I'll leave you to it, maybe we can meet this evening. I put on my blog an overdue post saying (as expatiated on in the last chapter) what a big part Gay is playing in Vic's Big Walk. I called the post Gay's Big Work.

Then Jacques was back again. While I wrote my blog, he was showing Gay round his land, of which there seemed to be quite a lot. Then he said he wanted to take us in his car to show us the other bits of his lands. He drove us round the area showing us this bit and that bit is mine and this forest is mine and that forest is mine, all over the place. He showed us the farm house his grandparents lived in. They used to own much of the area. It was very interesting. He showed us various splendid houses in the area. He said that Lussac-les-Chateaux, although it is named so, only has half a chateau, whereas Persac has seven chateaux. He showed us the big house of a man who he said was not rich at the beginning of the "last" war but was very rich at the end of it and nobody knows how this came about. I suppose everybody has a theory.

At one time Gay said something about Oradour, which is about 25 kms away and Jacques said Oh, do you want to go there? We nearly ended up in Oradour. We have been there before. It is a town which was completely destroyed, along with most of its population, by the Germans. It is now kept in that state as a monument and the new town of Oradour has sprung up beside it. You should go. It is a very dramatic illustration of man's cruelty to his own species, something which is unmatched in the "animal" world.

Eventually, well after six, we got back to Jacques' place and said we really must go and do our things – he had asked if we wanted to go for a drink before dinner – we said no, we really have to put the course into the Satmap and some other things. He said fine, I'll see you in the morning.

We no sooner had the maps out than he was back with his computer, saying can you show me how to connect to the Internet using the dongle. So I showed him that, which is good because it meant we were able to do something for him to repay his generosity. Clearly he is now going to get himself a dongle. Being here only some of the time, it is the ideal solution for him, as it is for me at the moment.

Jacques even invited us to visit him again, not only here in Persac, but also at his home in Montreal, Canada. A lovely, generous man. A pity we did not meet him when we were less pressed than on this trip.

It is forecast to be a hot day today. We got up at the usual time, about five, and I was on the road by half past six, hoping to get some walking in before the mercury climbs too far. Gay has dropped me off where she picked me up yesterday and I am immediately onto what was obviously an old railway track. I didn't realise at the time, but I was walking some of this yesterday.

First stop Lussac, which should be a coffee stop. I hadn't thought earlier, but now I text Gay to say shall we meet there to have coffee.

We were parked next to a frog pond last night – what a racket. I can't believe we have never noticed this in France before – maybe we thought it was something else or maybe we have never travelled at this time of the year. We certainly don't get it where we live.

Gay made Jacques laugh yesterday when he was giving us his guided tour. He was explaining that south of the Vienne, in the Languedoc, there are lots of towns ending in "ac". But there is not one north of the river. He stopped and pointed out a roadsign which gave directions to Lussac, Persac, Millac. Gay said "And there's another one – Tabac!" He laughed and complimented her sense of humour.

So, there is mist lying around everywhere, sun shining through the mist, birds twittering away, pigeons boring for Europe. Also that sort of purring sound which comes from some sort of critter which I have not managed to identify.

Forecast thunder and lightning tomorrow, and rain the day after. Back to the bad old days. After all, we have had three or four days of dry weather now.

As Gay predicted, walking along this railway track is a bit like my first day walking to Mirepoix, flat, trees on each side. I hope there are trees on each side later, when it gets hot, but I suspect not. I will be off the railway line for the last 20 kms.

At about 10 kms I meet Gay at Lussac-les-Chateaux. I have a nice croissant aux amandes and a grande crème. We realise we know Lussac. In fact we have stayed here several times, once at the very nice Orangerie hotel. The most memorable thing about that is that there were coracles floating in the swimming pool.

I am soon out in the countryside. Walking along roads with little shelter from the sun. Did Napoleon's armies not come this way? It is hot already. Forecast to be 28, but we have noticed that once the high temperatures are forecast, the actuality usually exceeds the forecast.

I have walked 21 kms now and it is, as predicted, hot. I am sweating like anything. The roads are quiet. They are very straight, but so quiet I feel able to listen to my iPod. I can actually hear any approaching vehicles behind, but I wouldn't use the iPod if the road was busy.

I have been listening to the speeches of Martin Luther King. I have a boxed set of CDs of his speeches which I haven't listened to before. Even his very first speech, a sermon actually, in Montgomery, the sermon in which he took up the civil rights challenge after Rosa Parks had been sent to jail for not giving up her seat on a bus to a white man. That first speech was electrifying.

The amazing thing about today's walk is that it is flat. I knew the first ten kms would be so, because it used to be a railway, but the other roads have been flat as well. It's the first flat day I have had since the very first day. This is the twenty second day. Not a bad average, a flat day once every three weeks.

We are skirting Poitiers to the east. I think after tomorrow's walk I will be north east of Poitiers. It looks a big city on the map. We have never been into the centre of it. I am glad we are not going too near on this trip. It would be a bit of a culture shock after the quiet places we have been frequenting.

At 24 kms I enter the little town of Chapelle-Viviers. Here I find another café and a rest for my legs. It is hard work in this heat, even with the roads being so flat. The man in the café, who doesn't say much else, despite the wonderful welcome described on the list of drinks on each table, tells me the temperature is 30 degrees. I think bloody hell, that's at half past eleven, what will it be like at three this afternoon? I tell him what I am doing and he gives me the French equivalent of "Oh, aye?"

I think it is the cheapest coffee I have ever seen in France, two euros. It always amazes us how expensive coffee or any drink is here, compared with Italy. Usually twice the price.

We finish up at Saint-Savin, although the finish of my walk today was 14 kms from here. This was the nearest campsite. St-Savin is twinned with Hartley Wintney, which could interest our friends who live there and possibly also the policeman who booked me for speeding outside the police college while my brother was lecturing inside.

The campsite is hosting a collection of campervans and caravans who are here to celebrate a 60th wedding anniversary. Tonight there will be feasting and accordion music. In town this afternoon there are celebrations of the 40th anniversary of the town being twinned with a German city. We shall walk into town presently and check that out – after all, I have walked a mere 30 kms today, giving a total so far of

683 kms to date.
We have seen donkeys every day. Of course they are cute, but I was wondering why they are there. After all, farmers do not keep any animal for sentimental reasons – they all have to earn their keep. We cleared this up with Jacques yesterday. The answer is simple, really. As that dog on the television used to say – Sausages!

Day 23. St. Savin to Pleumartin.

The 23rd day of my walk, which is supposed to finish on the 23rd day of next month. Is there any symmetry there?

Gay has dropped me off and it is about 6.30. A hare starts up in the field alongside me and tears away over the field. Stops, rears up, checks that I am really there, then charges away again. He doesn't know I am a vegetarian.

There are a lot more clouds this morning. It's also a bit windy, which is fine because it helps to keep me a bit cooler. But I think it is all part of the build-up to the storm which is supposed to arrive later. A thunder and lightning storm, that is.

I am walking back down the road which Gay just drove me along, from the campsite at St-Savin. As we were coming along in VFO I thought I saw a hoopoe flying up from the roadside. I would like to have a closer look at it. They are very fine looking birds, but with my eyesight they need to virtually sit on my knee before I can see them properly.

I have done about 5 kms when the rain starts – big, heavy drops. I get the cape out and put it on which immediately makes me uncomfortable because it is quite warm. I can hear thunder rumbling away upstairs. Fortunately not quite overhead at the moment and I hope it remains behind me.

The rain doesn't last too long, so off comes the poncho, although, looking at the sky, the rain could easily return.

I am about to enter a village called Lauthier, just as I am stowing my poncho away, when a pine marten runs across the road a few metres in front of me. Great. I wonder if it thinks the same of me?

I have walked 11.6 kms The thunder is still rumbling away, the sky is darkening and I am wondering if it is going to overtake me. Coming towards me is the first moving car I have seen today. Amazing traffic density.

The heavens open, the rain starts with a vengeance this time, so it is on with the poncho again. Just as I enter La Puye, the thunder and lightning starts, it seems overhead so escape seems in order. I was going to stop for a coffee anyway. I go to a boulangerie. I notice some pains aux raisins, 80 cents. I ask for one. She charges me 1.50. Am I being ripped off because I am a foreigner, or did I read the wrong label? They were rather small but the bag feels heavy. As I walk away, I realised I have two pains aux raisins, so of course I have to force them down.

I go to a bar and have a very strong coffee and the buns while sheltering from the rain. A man comes in on one of those motorised wheelchairs. He is obviously a serious paraplegic or worse. He can move barely a muscle. But he is also seriously friendly. As I am leaving, he says goodbye as I drop my Satmap and it comes apart. I think Christ, how am I going to get to Blackpool without this? He is concerned about whether it is broken. This could have been a disaster of major proportions because I am totally reliant on the Active 10 to find my way each day, after Gay has slaved over the maps the day before. I carry the maps with me as back-up but I am not sure what good they would be because I can't see the tracks, even with a magnifying glass (I carry one with me). Fortunately the Satmap isn't broken – it is the removable, replaceable screen which has come off the front and I manage to get it on again. Because of this, I have a bit of a chat with the wheelchair man and he is gobsmacked at what I am doing. All this makes me think about the contrast between, on the one hand, what is happening between me and this man and between this man and the other people, and on the other hand, the "does he take sugar" attitude – avoiding contact with a person's brain because his body is damaged.

There are a lot of signs up in the café for moto cross, and lots of trophies. I wonder whether the trophies are his and if he was a victim of an accident at this sport.

By the time I am ready to go the rain has stopped so I am able to walk away not wearing the poncho. I just carry it over my shoulder so it can dry out a bit. The lightning has passed away again for a while.

I am now on a long straight road which is the route to Chatellerault. Clear evidence that the Romans were here. I keep passing houses which have a sign saying "Maison Acadienne", a flag, with a star on blue, white, then orange vertical bars, a date 1774, and then below that another panel with another number, which varies, and two names, one male, one female, never the same surname.

I have also seen the phrase "la ligne Acadienne" more than once and a house being done up with the word "Acagite" and a website www.acagite.fr, both on the builder's board. I wonder if this is something to do with the Arcadians, who went to Canada –were they a persecuted minority? – then to Louisiana, where they became the Cajuns, who have donated their music and food to the world.

So fascinated am I by this ligne Acadienne, that I suddenly realise I am following it instead of my route. I have gone 3.7 kms past where I should have turned right. Bloody hell. I turn back. Fortunately, I can use the Satmap to get me out of that one. Instead of going back all the way to where I went wrong I cut across country via various lanes to a point where I can meet the track I should have been on. I don't know how many kms that has added to my journey today – 2 or 3, I would say.

I eventually pull into Pleumartin, which has an enormous central square, where Gay is waiting for me with V-Force One. There is no campsite here so we drive on to La-Roche-Posay. At last a bit of camouflage! There are so many geriatrics here that nobody will notice me. It is a spa town, full of hotels and apartments which cater, as the spas do, to people taking the waters, which is something which is paid for by the national health service in France. There are also plenty of restaurants so I think I will take ma honey out tonight.

Today's walk was 32 kms, giving 715 to date.

Day 24. Pleumartin to Abilly.

Comme toujours, I am moving on. Moving On was a Hank Snow song with a driving rythym, also recorded by Elvis. Did you know that Hank Snow, as well as being a real rhinestone cowboy of extremely limited height from his cowboy boots to his wig, was also the main financial backer of Elvis' career? The "colonel" didn't invest – he only collected.

I leave the bells of Pleumartin banging away behind me and head north. I have gone less than 2 kms when I see some fallow deer in a field on my right. I think they may be tame. If not, the farmer will be wondering who is demolishing his bales of hay. I get some photos of the deer.

What a palaver it was getting some electricity at last night's campsite in La-Roche-Posay. The prises, which we are supposed to plug into, and which we paid for, were four campervan emplacements away. We have the normal extension cable but it wouldn't reach that far. Gay went to see madame to say have you got an extension or should we move. Madame said she would speak to her husband. Two hours later, there was no progress with this, and no electricity. Gay went to see her again and got the immortal line, "I was just thinking about you and the fact that I have done nothing."

An extension cable was duly provided but all the bits did not fit together. All the men at the other campers became involved, this is what you do, et cetera. Unspoken thought, women can't be trusted with this sort of thing. Eventually, even as men they retired defeated and we had to wait for the husband of madame to arrive with yet more pieces and eventually we got some electricity. We woke up this morning and found that we no longer had a supply. But neither was there any light in the facilities block, so maybe the power is cut off at night in case somebody uses it.

It was a busy campsite and everybody seemed to know everybody else, like a small village. As Gay said, they were probably all taking the waters. As far as we could see, looking at the price lists at the hotels, taking the waters involves a course of about 24 days, so if they have to stay that long, no wonder they all know each other.

I am a bit tired this morning, which is unfortunate because I am told this is going to be a long day of 34 kms. I know that when I first started VBW all the stages were of that length. But lately, thanks to Gay's replanning, they have all been at or under 30 kms. Even yesterday should have been so, but that was my own foolishness and fascination with the Cajuns which made it 32. Also, it is humid this morning after yesterday's rain. It started off cool, but it has soon warmed up. Humidity always helps to sap the strength.

The terrain has changed again here. Open fields. I wouldn't say it is flat, just more rolling. When Jacques Felix was driving us round the Persac area so proudly the other day, he was pointing out the small fields in that area, with hedges, and how much he preferred them to the big open fields, even though he realised the latter are more efficiently farmed. That was two days ago, and here we are, completely different again. Big fields. And of course there are always woods. There is so much woodland in France.

A lovely building on the right. La Vervolviere. A historic monument. Part chateau, part house. Beautiful.

Coussay-les-Bois. Don't know if they will have coffee here. Too early for a coffee stop? No matter, I can't find a bar. I was looking at the war memorial in the centre of this town. About 30 dead in the First World War, from this small town, not much more than a village. What a terrible event that was. Not many named for the Second World War, mind. Two dead and two deported, which usually means sent to the death camps.

At 14 kms I arrive at Lesigny-sur-Creuse. A funny place. It is big enough to have a pharmacy and a boulangerie, but no bar, or certainly not one open on a Monday. The woman in the boulangerie tells me that at Maire, a couple of kms down the road, there is a bar open every day. It is on my route. Sure enough there is a bar, despite the village being much smaller than Lesigny. Unfortunately, I do not have time for a detour to the nearby village of Angles-sur-l'Anglin. That would be worth it, just for the name.

I cross the river Creuse at la Guerche. This immediately puts me in a different département and a different region. The registration plates on the parked cars tell the story – 37 instead of 86. I am in Indre-et-Loire from Vienne, and the region is Centre whereas on the other side of the river it was Poitou Charente. This means changing the mapping card in my Satmap device, and this in turn emphasises that I am making progress, or moving on, as above.

I walk on to Abilly. We are north of Poitiers now. I have walked 29 kms for the day instead of the threatened 34. I have now done, in VBW, 744 kms. A few small but stiff climbs gave me total ascents of not much over 700 metres – a doddle. The campsite is very pleasant. Like a park. And we have it all to ourselves.

Today I was struck by how many immense houses I saw, or chateaux, still in good condition, and many seemingly still in private hands.

Day 25. Abilly to Nouatre.

At six kms I find myself in the town of Descartes. It's the biggest town I have seen so far, I think. The chief export is philosophy. It seems a bit large and too industrialised to suit a philosopher. Mind you, quoting Descartes, or mentioning his name, has become a bit of an industry in itself, and of course Descartes made into the famous Monty Python Philosophers' Drinking Song in the line:
And Rene Descartes was a drunken fart:
"I drink, therefore I am"
Renaming the town has been a bit of a growth industry as well. Originally called La Haye en Tourraine, it was renamed La Haye-Descartes in 1802 in his honour. The final morphing into plain and simple old Descartes took place in 1967.

I have just seen and eaten something I have never seen in France before. I went into a boulangerie in Descartes and saw they had pattes des ours – bears' paws. We have seen these in the United States, where they call them bear claws. Except that the French type are not covered in sweet icing sugar like those in America. And they were very nice – I use the plural advisedly because once again I seemed to end up with two.

I don't know if Descartes was into bears' claws, but he believed that man is born free and that everything is a result of choice – you have a choice in everything. Nevertheless, he had several overriding principles so that the whole thing didn't descend into anarchy. A belief in a supreme being was one. I'm not so sure about that one. Another principle was that one should obey the laws of the state. There were other sub-clauses, but you get the idea.

Pretty much my own philosophy. I get really annoyed when people say to me, "Aren't you lucky because you can do this and that and the other". Almost always they are referring to something I do that they don't do, but which has been a matter of choice, of decisions and priorities, rather than of luck. Almost always they do something and spend money on something which I don't do. For instance that I can afford to give up my job and try something else, which I have done several times. As it happens it has worked out OK. But it could just as easily have gone the other way. I took a risk and went on from there. And applied myself 100%, as I am doing with this walk. The one I find particularly annoying is, "Aren't you lucky to able to go abroad on holiday? I couldn't afford it. You must have a money tree". That last particular phrase came from someone who, at the time he said it, spent far more per year on cigarettes than I did on holidays. And he had been smoking since he was a kid. I went on my first holiday abroad when I was 46. Most of my contemporaries were well accustomed to having their holidays abroad years before that. Do not covet thy neighbour's ass.

I have been walking only 18 kms. Pretty flat, pleasant but uninteresting countryside. I have reached a sign saying "Nouatre", which is the town I am heading for. I understood Nouatre was going to be at 26 kms. This is excellent, I think.

I check on the trusty Satmap and find I still have about 5 kms to go to the meeting point. Within one kilometre I am passing a "goodbye Nouatre" sign. I must be cutting corners of the commune because before long I am coming round into Nouatre again from another direction. The first bit must have been a tongue of it sticking out into the countryside.

I have been listening on my iPod to more speeches by Martin Luther King. Very impressive. The man was only in his thirties when he was killed. He was in his twenties when he made the speeches I am listening to, in the mid 1950s.

I have a bit of trouble with the arthritis in the ball of my left foot. It is making me hobble – am I going to hobble for 2000 kms?

I find Gay waiting for me in the centre of Nouatre. We are encamped at Ste-Maure-de-Tourraine, a few kms away. This town has a cheese named after it. It was a short walk of 24 kms. Total distance covered to date is 768 kms. Next Wednesday I will probably go over the 1000 kms mark. What sort of celebration should we have for that?

—

How many roads must a man walk down …?

Thank you, Bob, very philosophical, in keeping with a day which included Descartes, but I don't think people will buy that sort of dirgy stuff.

Various people have taken a stab at suggesting theme songs for Vic's Big Walk. Most of them have been fairly obvious, – These Boots Were Made For Walking – I Walk The Line – On The Road Again. But nobody has suggested this Bob Dylan number, or, for instance, Maura o'Connell's Footsteps Fall. I ask on my blog for suggestions.

Day 26. Nouatre to Panzoult.

Less than a kilometre into today's walk I am very nearly mowed down by a boy on a bicycle who comes round a corner at high speed just as I am turning the same corner and about to step into the road because the pavement has terminated. He is very close to me, and I don't mean dear to my heart. Late for school I suppose. I have been knocked down by a bike before and it is no joke. I was lying in the road last time, unconscious and surrounded by a Practorian guard of Altrincham lady athletes. It was almost worth the parrot features which ensued from the fat lip and swollen nose.

I don't know if we have moved out of frog territory. I haven't heard any for a couple of days. We certainly haven't moved out of cuckoo territory. They are cuckooing away. We even had one, when we were in Abilly, which took up residence, in full voice, outside the van just after we had gone to bed. I don't know which is more boring, a cuckoo or a pigeon.

At Parçay-sur-Vienne I go into a boulangerie for a croissant or something, and watch the person before me buy up every one in the place.

I cross the river, which is very wide now. This is when I realise I am going in the wrong direction. I shouldn't have crossed the Vienne at all. I get the brown roads mixed up with the different brown line which is my route on the screen of my Satmap. As well as the other problems with my eyes, I have always been bad on colour. So, back over the bridge, over the Vienne. Which gives me the opportunity to find out that I haven't left the frogs behind – there are plenty by the river bank.

I can see how I missed the turn. What I took to be the entrance of a hotel car park turns out to be the beginning of a track which runs parallel with the river.

I seem to be in the bread basket of France. It is flattish country. Everywhere is grain, various types – wheat, barley, corn just starting to grow – obviously a later crop.

The coffee I had in Parçay was the cheapest I have ever had in France, at 1.50 Euros. Almost down to Italian levels. It has been cheaper in this area, but in Italy you would get a bun included for that price. I have noticed that hereabouts, for a grand crème, they usually give you the milk separately, and cold. In one place I was at a couple of days ago, they gave me a big cup of strong coffee, with one of those tiny plastic tubs of milk, which hardly made a difference to its colour.

I go past a village called Beauvais, which I am sure figures in the historical novels, such as those Gay is reading at the moment by Sharon Penman. I am on GR48 again and I am still not seeing any other walkers.

I come up to a chateau on my left, which is the Chateau Rolandiere. Unfortunately, when I get near enough to photograph it, there are high stone walls and hedges and I can't see a thing. I come to a gate where I think I may get a picture and, blow me down, there is a caravan site inside the walls. It looks pretty much well occupied. If we had known about this, we could have been in there for tonight, chateau-ed up and with lots of potential prosylisees available.

I walk along the river Vienne again, at the village of Mougon. A man says, "You are marching very well!" I haven't had that for a while. So I stop and explain to the old man (I must stop saying that – I sometimes realise when I have said it that the man was probably younger than me) what I am doing. He shakes my hand and says, "Felicitations! Et bonne courage!" I really should carry the Pancreatic Cancer collecting tin with me.

Good heavens! Somebody walking towards me. But not a randonneur. He is not carrying anything. He is just out for a local stroll. False alarm – I thought the GR was being used for its purpose.

I am north of St Gilles. Gay is camped up and is walking back to meet me on the agreed route, but the agreed route doesn't exist. I am looking for a left turn which isn't there. I can see, on my Satmap, ways round it, but Gay may choose a different solution. Thank goodness for text messages. She agrees to wait at a spot till I come round to it, by heading north, west, south, then west again.

We end up on a farm (camping a la ferme), which is actually a winery, where I get a surprisingly good signal on my dongle, and a free service today for some reason. Gay gets a couple of bottles of wine, one rose and one red, to try another time. The wine of the region is chenin, rouge et blanc.

Today I was musing that what I am doing is not all that unusual, or rather it was not, until recently. Before armies became mechanised, which really happened only during the Second World War, it was the norm for bodies of men to march huge distances, carrying heavy equipment. "The enemy is 800 kms away. Quick! March over there and have a battle!" "Oh no! Whoops! They outsmarted us – they are where we started from – hurry back there! Just another 800 kms. "

Mind you, I don't suppose many of them were a few weeks away from being 70 years of age. The old men were at home, starting the wars to which they would send the young men. Or sitting on horses, collecting medals and titles, having already seized the high ground so they could have a good view.

We are near Panzoult. Distance today 27 kms. To date 795 kms.

Day 27. Panzoult to Chinon.

Is this the reason for the sudden change from cereal production to vines yesterday? I seem to have moved from the flatness of the last few days to some fairly steep hills. Much more suitable for men with secateurs than it is for combine harvesters.

It's trying to rain on me a bit here, which is not much fun. At least it means the temperature is not going to go high. That's a decent price to pay.

I stop off in the village of Cravant les Coteaux for a coffee and a pain aux raisins. Just before I get there I see quite a few houses that are caves with house fronts. Including one that looks quite classy. Unfortunately, I couldn't really take a picture of it because a man was just coming out. Some people don't take too kindly to you standing there photographing their house.

While listening to Dr. King's "I have a dream" speech, I am not paying enough attention to my navigation. So when I am north of Chinon and the GR splits into two, I head north for more than a kilometre, instead of heading south into Chinon, before I realise I have gone wrong.

I retrace my footsteps. At the point where I went wrong, there is a squad of soldiers. I'm not sure what is happening. One looks as if he is having a medal pinned to him. Or maybe the officer is sewing his buttons for him. They all have guns and they have an ambulance with them. I saw military vehicles zooming about in the woods some time ago.

I am now about half an hour behind schedule. Gay is already at the rendezvous point, but I have done over 22 kms and need a rest and a coffee in Chinon. Chinon figures in the book which I started reading yesterday. In fact the very next chapter takes place in Chinon. It is one of Sharon Penman's excellent historical novels about the Angevin kings of England, who were also usually the rulers of various bits of France, although that changes a bit from chapter to chapter and battle to battle.

The soldiers are following me down this hill. They are not catching up, it has to be said. I glance over my shoulder to see where the soldiers are and notice they have turned off. This is when I realise I have done it again –I should have turned off at the same point.

There is another bunch of soldiers coming down so after course correction I am between the two of them. It's like having an escort. It is strange that only yesterday I made the comment about soldiers on the march.

Chinon seems quite a big place. I am marching along high above it for quite a while. Down below it the town is all modern buildings, then, when I get nearer to the centre, it becomes much older. I come down hill. I pass and spurn one of those lifts that takes you down from one street to another. The road ahead of me is dug up and a man tells me I can't go down there, even on foot. So in fact I do have to use the lift. This takes me right down into the centre. I have to go through a tunnel into a square where there are a number of restaurants and cafes so I get myself a cup of coffee there. I still have about 4 kms to go. Some posey writer types are yah-yahing at the next table. I get the impression they are on a course.

The route takes me across a bridge over a river, which is again the Vienne. Does this mean I am in the Languedoc again?

I'm soon out in the country again and the sky is darkening up. I hear the ominous rumble of thunder. I am in for another soaking, not the first today.

True enough, I soon have to get the poncho out again. It's already wet. But I need it, the downpour is heavy. And just as I reach where Gay has parked down a narrow lane, the thunder becomes overhead, deafening and threatening.

We are a few kms past Chinon, although our camp is ahead in Candes-St-Martin. We shall have to come back in the morning for me to pick up the thread.

Today's tramp was 30 kms. 825 in all now. And after 3 days of flatter land, I am back to steeper work, with total ascents today of 1257 metres.

Day 28, Chinon to Allonnes.

Another wet day. It takes me 3 hours to get back to Candes-St-Martin, where we had spent the night. Soon after that, I am crossing the immensely long bridge over the

Loire at Montsoreau, I am surrounded by seagulls, which is a strange feeling, not having heard one for many a month.

I miss out in Montsoreau. Gay had said before I started today that there would be a choice of coffee stops. I don't see any until I get to Montsoreau, which is about halfway. She had sent me a text which said Montsoreau looked a good place for a coffee stop, just before the bridge, good for walkers. So I get to Montsoreau and there are lots of cafes. But I walk past them all, looking for the one which is near the bridge and is good for walkers. When I get to the bridge the coffee shops are well behind me. What she meant is that Montsoreau is good for coffee stops, it is just before the bridge, and the bridge is good for walkers – this is the bridge which we had worried about, wondering whether it had passage for pedestrians, because if so, it cuts off many a kilometre from the GR route.

The bridge does have pedestrian passages on each side, but I find out later that the bridge is not good for battlebuses. It has a width restriction, which you don't find out until you are committed. Gay bashed one of our huge wing-mirrors to pieces, with all its innards hanging out. She managed to put it together again but is unsure whether the electrics will work.

After talk of it being a good day for coffee stops, here I am, 18 kms into today's walk, and I haven't had one yet. I eventually find one in Varennes-sur-Loire.

Having crossed the Loire, I am now in a different region, Pays de la Loire instead of Centre, and a different département, Maine et Loire instead of Indre et Loire.

I head for Allonnes. Gay is picking me up in the centre, having found the campsite is 3 kms out of town. It is now a completely different agricultural area. There is some corn, but mainly market gardens and fruit. Flat as well.

When I get to the church in Allonnes, where Gay and I had agreed to meet, she is not there. It's not much fun standing around when you have walked two thirds of a marathon, but there is nowhere to sit. And the sun has just come onto the boil after the inevitable daily rain. It isn't long before she drives up in V-Force One. It appears that the campsite, 3 kms outside Allonnes, where she has already booked in, is locked up between 12 and 2, and they were reluctant to let her out. Are these places for the benefit of the public, or are they prisons? They admonished her not to come back before 2, so we sit outside the gates and have our lunch.

Today's walk was 28.5 kms, with a mere 995 metres of ascents. 853.5 kms so far.

I have received more suggestions of theme songs for VBW. One which has come into my head – I can't imagine why – is "The Long And Winding Road".

Chapter 11. The Fifth Week

Day 29. Allonnes to Parçay-le-Pins

On my way from Allonnes to la Breille-les-Pins, which is about 9 kms, the first stage of today's walk, and probably the only place I will get a coffee. I have gone back to wearing the shoes I set out in, after 3 weeks using the old ones. The newer pairs are fine. Clearly the problem was not with the shoes but that my feet were swollen through mistreatment and my own foolishness.

I pass a mediaeval park, which looks interesting, reconstructed villages from the Middle Ages and the like.

We had a very pleasant visit yesterday afternoon from Judith and Rob Fletcher, who made a big detour to see us instead of going straight from Calais to their house in the Creuse. In the evening, they came again from Breille to drive us back to their hotel for an excellent meal. This was extremely splendid just to look at. It seemed a shame to disturb it but heroically we pressed on and ate it. Rob then drove us back to our camp in Allonnes, where we said goodbye, for now. This morning I realised that I would be passing by their hotel on my walk, and that in fact it was the only chance of a coffee stop today.

I arrive a few minutes after they have departed. But I have a nice chat with two English couples who are still breakfasting. Of course I tell them about VBW and they immediately come up with a donation, which I later put onto the JustGiving website on their behalves. Thanks go to Joyce and Tony, Ann and Fred.

An uneventful walk to Parçay-le-Pins from la Breille, mainly through woodlands, as it was also from Allonnes to la Breille. I see very few people all day. I also see very little traffic because I walk mainly on tracks which, fortunately, are not mountainous.

I march into Parçay-le-Pins, where Gay is waiting in V-Force One, right underneath the very loud church bells which I have heard from several kilometres away. Because the drive to a campsite is another 10 kms, we nip into the local café/bar. When Gay asks for tea, mine host reveals himself to be English, and named Terry. He refuses payment for the two drinks. The price will go into the purple PCUK collecting tin we have for that purpose – it now contains a number of small amounts for little kindnesses such as Terry's – it will be emptied eventually and the proceeds put onto JustGiving as a collective donation. Terry is also going to display details of VBW and the need for donations, in his bar. Thanks, Terry.

Today's walk was 25 kms. Total to date 878. Today's climbing practice was 813 metres.

These are some of the Vic's Big Walking Songs, with additional comments where appropriate) suggested so far by readers of my blog:
- I Walk The Line – Johnny Cash
- These Boots Were Made For Walking – Nancy Sinatra
- Walk On By – Dionne Warwick
- Running On Empty – Jackson Browne
- Anything by The Walker Brothers or Junior Walker and The All Stars.
- Run For Home – Lindisfarne
- On The Road Again – Willie Nelson
- Keep Right On To The End Of The Road – Sir Harry Lauder
- You'll Never Walk Alone
- Just Walking In The Rain (how appropriate)
- Where'er You Walk
- Walk The Road Again – Rod King liked this title because it is appropriately included in a song collection book named 'The Coffee House Songbook'
- Walk On The Wild Side
- Walk Don't Run
- Walking On Sunshine
- Walking In The Sunshine
- Walking In Rhythm
- Walking For That Cake (Yes, really! This title is included in a songbook named 'Best Loved Songs Of The American People' – I wonder why?)
- My Shoes Keep Walking Back To You (This song is specially for you (Vic), to sing to Gay and should be Columbia's favourite)
- Take Me Home Country Roads.
- Hit the road, Jack
- Dale Heighway gave me the full words for "Manchester Rambler" and "Thirsty Boots"
- John Hayfield came up with: "Walk & Don't Look Back "
- I'm Walking, Yes, Indeed I'm Walking, by Fats Domino

Nobody, including me, suggested the one which the BBC eventually used in a news item about the walk finish. One which should have been immediately obvious. Walk Of Life, by Dire Straits. This walk is the walk of my life, it is a walk to save lives, and it is one of my favourite records.

Jean Dolan e-mailed me:

I've just read today's news but you don't tell us how you are feeling. Are you tired, do your feet hurt, what do you think about? Such long hours all on your own, it's a good job you've got Gay. Good man Vic. Step you gaily. xxxxx

I repeat the question on my blog which is where I post this answer.

Quite right, Jean, I have not reported lately on how I am feeling.

I have been walking for 29 days. I feel fairly tired towards the end of each walk, and don't feel like doing much for the rest of the day. It's just the legs that feel as if they have done something – apart from that I am not particularly tired or sleepy. I could probably do with a masseur for my legs. I am sleeping no more than usual and by the next morning do not feel any residual tiredness

I gave myself a problem with my feet in the first week, which has left my big toe and the one next to it on the left foot both with nails now hanging off. I also have arthritis in the big toe joint on the left foot – I have had it for a while, but only intermittently – now I have it all the time – I don't know if that will subside after VBW. My right foot is fine – maybe I should just hop?

Apart from that, everything seems to be in working order, no problems of any kind.

Mentally I am not having a problem. I haven't even thought much about how on earth I got involved in such a huge physical commitment. I haven't even gloated much over the fact that this is something which nobody else, in the history of man, has ever done, walking from Puivert to Blackpool, never mind at the age of 70. But I have noticed that it is a long way, and that I am not halfway there yet.

What do I think about? Maybe I should be thinking deep thoughts, but I am not. I expected to spend much of the time ruminating on my life and how I got to where I am now. Maybe that will happen more when I get to England and visit places which remind me of various phases of my life.

I spend a lot of time just enjoying the pleasure of the quiet highways and byways, the silence, apart from bird and animal sounds, the lack of traffic almost every day.

I also spend quite a lot of time wondering whether there will be a coffee place in the next town, if it will be open, and whether I can have a few minutes rest, which is amazingly rejuvenating.

I am dictating extensively as I walk, getting on for 2,000 words a day, which may possibly form the basis of a book. Of course that also has to be transcribed every evening.

I listen a bit to my iPod, which has about 700 albums on it, but I have mainly listened to language courses and am enjoying listening to the speeches of Martin Luther King.

So I am indeed stepping me gaily, and hope to continue to do so for another 41 days.

An anonymous comment on my blog says;

Vic, you really are an incredible inspiration. I think it says a lot when someone strips their life down to the bare essentials and spends so much time with themselves I imagine it's a very interesting process, rumination or not.

You are hugely inspiring and to put it bluntly, you're a hero.

Regardless of why you're doing it, for whatever cause, the task itself is monumental and your dedication is incredible. Proof that it's never too late, we're never too old and we can all accomplish something meaningful in our lifetime.

Best wishes to Gay as well, as she is also an incredible force in all this and it speaks of her character and passion to be so involved.

May you both be well, may you both have ease of mind, and may you both continue to have strength of spirit.

I have had this word "hero" aimed at me a few times, comments on my blog, e-mails, messages accompanying donations on JustGiving, and on Facebook. I find it very embarrassing.

Day 30. Parçay-le-Pins to Broc.

Sunday morning. I have walked 10 kms and, as I am entering Noyant, I see two interesting things. One is a rat, in broad daylight, scurrying away from a waste bin outside a restaurant – not one of those stinky bins full of last nights leavings, just a little waste bin on a pole. Next to the restaurant is a hairdresser which is offering a free travelling hairdryer to anybody who has two shampoos, which seems a good deal. Depends how much a shampoo costs, of course. We don't have a hairdryer in the house at home, or even in the little house on wheels. We both have short hair, which dries itself very quickly.

I have coffee in Noyant. As I am leaving the town, standing at a crossroads, I feel as if I am in the pages of a history book. The signposts say Angers, Tours, and Blois. All places which figure very much in English/French history, along with battles, wars, brutal sudden death and kings.

Gay picks me up at La Barberie, near Broc and takes us to Le Lude, which must be quite near to Le Mans, because there are lots of signs to Le Mans and lots of enthusiasts running round in old cars. The 24-hour races are on this weekend.

It is a nice town, with a large and magnificent chateau with vast grounds. This belongs to the Count and Countess Louis-Jean de Nicolaÿ. It has been in the same family for 250 years, so it seems that both the family and the property survived the French Revolution. How did that come about?

We go out for a pizza, accompanied by some wine called Chateau Caroline. We think it would be good to get hold of a bottle of this because when, in a few weeks time, we stay in Reading with friends Rod and Caroline, it would be quite droll to produce it. But we fail to find any in the shops.

A quiet day, with nothing much to report. The only matters of note are:

1.   I passed the 900 kms mark, having walked 28 kms today, 906 kms in all so far. Total ascents today 874 metres.

2.   It was dry. This is possibly the fifth day out of 30 in which I have not been wet while walking. I should make the most of it because the forecast for the next 3 days, which is as far as it goes in the newspaper, is wet.

Day 31. Broc to Mayet.

Not a single coffee stop today. True to the forecast, it started raining just before we got up. We did that slightly later than usual, because the campsite gate wasn't going to be unlocked until 7 so there didn't seem to be any point being up at 5 and ready to go by 6.

I see a sign outside a house – Bastard Olivier – painter and decorator. They are very blunt in France, aren't they?

I cross the Loir and walk alongside it for a while. This is a tributary of the Loire. At one stage there is a gite which is a little different because it is also a historic monument, a paper mill. The panneau invites you to come and look around but also people will be lodging there, which makes it a bit awkward.

Apart from that, the walk is country roads, little traffic, birds, dogs – the usual, nothing much interesting to report. And certainly no bloody coffee stops, either.

When I was answering Jean's question the other day, I omitted to say that, although I am not generally very tired, some days I am more tired than others. This was such a day. The day's walk was only 24 kms (have you noticed how Gay's excellent navigation has cut my average day down from about 35 to 30, by including some days well under 30, although we still end up in the same place as previously planned?) and thank goodness it was no further. I was dragging my feet from very early on. I have had days like this before, and will probably be back to normal tomorrow.

We are in Mayet, having completed 930 kms so far. Tomorrow we shall land up even closer to Le Mans, and we are having some trouble finding a campsite, but as usual Gay comes good.

Day 32. Mayet to Ruaudin.

This is a good start to the 32nd day. The campsite at Mayet is in a park, with a biggish fishing lake. The campsite is locked up, as usual, which is fine because we knew that, and there are little escape hatches round the barrier for pedestrians. My route takes me round the lake, to the other side of the park, where the gate is locked. I think of climbing over, but may do myself an injury, so I have to come back. What's the point of having a gate locked at one end of the park when you can walk in and out at the other end?

It is 15th June, it's like a winter's day. It's forecast to rain again. It gave a little foretaste before I set off. It's windy, it's cold, it's grey. I could be in England.

One of the things I have noticed throughout France, apart from frogs and dogs and cuckoos and crickets, is the complete lack of somewhere for the weary traveller to sit for a few minutes. As I have said, I like to break up each walk into about 3 sections by having a rejuvenating 5 or 10 minute break. If I can find a coffee shop that's fine because it forces me to take that length of time, but out in the country, I don't think I have seen one place where there has been a seat by the roadside or at a junction. There are some in towns, but in towns there is usually a coffee shop anyway. And I look, so I know they are not there. There aren't even many places where there is a raised bank at the side of the road, which is sittable-on, or where there have been raised banks it has been when it has been throwing it down. Who wants to sit on a wet bank in the rain? My fertile (or is it febrile?) brain begins to conceive the Plonk-It seat, of which more later.

So many things are regionalised. In this area, for example, in many of the gardens there are small, round structures, which are generally quite old, with a little door. I thought, could they be outside toilets, but they are too small. You would have to be a gnome to get in, and they would be so claustrophobic inside. Gay says they are called puit (she is not sure and Wikipedia is not much help) and that they are to cover wells.

I reach a town which dare not say its name. I have certainly not seen a sign, which is unusual. It's a biggish town, with a busy main road running through it. I could cross this road and carry on up the GR, or I go into the town to find a coffee and bun.

There is a market, so I text Gay, who has not left Mayet. Unusually, she is not in advance of me because I was able to walk straight from the campsite and did not need to be dropped anywhere, whereas she was trapped. I eventually find the name of the town Eccomoy. I have seen the word a few times but thought it was a dyslexic version of economy. Gay loves markets and we have encountered not a decent one in the past month, just a couple with only a few stalls.

Some time later I reach a funny place, at 20 kms – there are 2 boulangeries, but no bar. What sort of place has two bakers but no bar? Clearly the people of Teloché have to eat their croissants in the silence of their lonely rooms.

The arthritis in the ball of my left foot, which intermittently bothered me, but not much, for some time before the walk, has now become persistent. I can feel it with every footfall, or every left footfall. I don't know whether this is because I am whacking it so much; whether it will subside once I have finished VBW or if I am stuck with it. Or indeed whether anything can be done about it.

Just near the end of the walk I pass a man training his horse and sulky. Round and round a track. A private track? Sulky racing, or trotting, is quite widespread in France.

At this point I realise that the track I am following has disappeared. There is one marked on the map but in reality it becomes a field full of crops. I can see a house on the other side of the field. I could possibly walk round the edge of the field but could end up in somebody's garden and they wouldn't be too pleased. I am only about 300 metres short of the finish. I can see a road with traffic off to my left so walk round the edge of another field and come to the road, except that there is a barrier of bracken, which is not too bad, but it is also full of nettles. I find a place which is not too nettley, push through, and find a ditch, which I have to jump over to reach the road. I didn't expect to still be doing this sort of thing near the end of my 70th year.

Gay is waiting for me near Ruaudin and we whizz off to Yvres l'Eveque, some distance away, the nearest campsite, which is a very modern one.

Today I walked past a place called Vatican, so it's no wonder VBW feels like a long way. I walked 29 kms, with a climb of 1014 metres. Total kms to date are 959.

The threatened rain was feeble in its approaches today and did not occasion the donning of a waterproof poncho. But again the temperature did not struggle out of the teens. These temperatures are fine for me, but the people of France are clearly wondering where their summer is this year.

I think I may have forgotten to say that last Friday, when I crossed the Loire, I also left Centre Region for Pays de la Loire. We are still in that region, Sarthe département. In a very few days, we shall be in our final region of France, Normandy, and will be preparing for the invasion of England.

Day 33. Ruaudin to Neuville-sur-Sarthe

This day dawns bright and sunny, for a change. The temperature inside the vehicle is only 11. God knows what it is outside. I find out when I start walking that not only is it cold, but the wind, which we thought had died away, has not. It has just changed direction so that we were sheltered on the campsite. I am certainly not sheltered from it now. This is a cold, cold wind. I remind myself that it is 5 days before the sun turns round to go back south of the Equator.

I had been tempted to just wear the t-shirt and not my jacket. I'm glad I didn't do that.

A rabbit dashes away between the trees. My walks are still very largely rural but I have been seeing the odd sign that I am in the more populated, industrialised north. At Eccomoy yesterday there was a big chemical plant, just outside the town. I am seeing more busy roads with fast traffic. Fortunately these are roads that I have to cross rather than walk along.

I walk today from Ruaudin, where I finished yesterday, through Yvrés l'Evêque (where we spent last night), to near Neuville-sur-Sarthe. We are in an area of many horses. They obviously breed them round here. Is there anything more beautiful than a horse, except for a baby horse? I have just passed one "Poney Club" and texted Gay that I am 2 kms from the rendezvous, when I find myself wading through what looks like the Amazon delta. This is the worst bit of track I have come across in almost 1,000 kms. Liquid mud, over a kilometre of it, the track being too narrow to escape onto the side, and the mud stirred by lots of cycle tracks. This slows me down a bit, makes me, as Billy Connolly would say "skite about" and makes a right mess of my shoes.

The campsite at Neuville where we had planned to spend the rest of the day is closed, so Gay has found another one, on a farm, at La Guiérche. The farm people say that the other campsite has been taken over by some Brits and promptly closed.

The day remains dry, but continues very cold. The coldest day since I started VBW. The temperature just before I started out, 11 degrees Celsius, was inside a V-Force One, which had been heated all night by two two-legged portable 2KW heaters. So outside it must have been much less. This lack of heat was being pushed from the North East by a strong wind. I blame Putin for all this. I have never liked him – or anyone called Vladimir, for that matter. The name didn't get off to a good start with that Impaler fellow, did it?

More songs have been suggested. Nicola's favourite is the already-suggested "Take me home, country roads". I like that one as well, especially as I have been known to play it in public (as part of a large band), but the trouble I have with it is that I don't feel as if I am walking home. I know I am walking back through my life to the root of it all, but I feel very strongly that Puivert is my home, not Blackpool.

Another one Nicola suggests, for when I reach the channel, is Neil Diamond's "Walk on Water". Which reminds me – I have perfected a groan which emerges when somebody, learning about VBW, says, with an air of "Caught you out!" – "So what will you do when you reach the channel?" What do you think I will do? I'm not going to swim across, am I? Then it is implied that I should walk round and round the ship until it lands, and that somehow I am cheating if I do not do so. Well, I'm not cheating, because I make the rules up for this unique event, but the real answer is – "If you say you are driving to England, does that mean that you are going to drive round and round the ferry until it reaches the other shore?"

Valerie, perhaps remembering that Gay and I go by different routes to the same point each day, has suggested "You take the high road and I'll take the low road". And there is a Scottish connection – the day after VBW finishes on my 70th birthday, we shall be in Scotland for a week or more.

Leslie Stephens, who says he is a much younger man than me – because his 70th birthday falls 8 days after mine – suggests that, in view of the weather I have had for most of this trip, "Walking in the rain" would be very appropriate. It has already been suggested, but how true!

After a 24 kms march, my total is 983 kms. A mere 910 metres of climb today.

Day 34. Neuville-sur-Sarthe to Assé-le-Riboul

Thursday. Dry as I set out. Still very cool. Not the wind there was yesterday. Forecast to rain later but OK at the moment. The first 8 kms of my walk sees me back in la Guiérche, which is where we spent the night on a very quiet farm camp. I pause in la Guiérche for coffee, then march on through Souillé.

I'm walking mainly on GR36 now. This is the one that takes me almost to the ferry ramp – it actually goes to Ouistreham, which is the port for Caen. But I have yet to see another walker on the GR36. I was told it was the M1 of Grandes Randonnées, and yet I have not seen a single walker on it. In fact it is weeks since I saw another walker of any kind. The last people I saw who could be construed as walkers were the soldier boys who escorted me into Chinon, and that was a week ago. But of recreational walkers, I have seen nary a one for at least two weeks, maybe three.

As I am entering a small but busy town, certainly in terms of traffic, called Sainte-Jamme-sous-Sarthe, Karen rings me from Saudi Arabia. I haven't seen Karen, or any of my daughters, this year, as they are scattered to the four winds and three continents. I stop and sit on a wall, thinking if I have a signal I had better not move to a worse place. But sure enough we do lose the signal a couple of times, so the third time she rings I just carry on walking and then we are not cut off at all. I walk out of the town. She is on the phone for nearly an hour which is very nice. She tells me that the temperature is in the mid 40s, Celsius. Also that when she went out with friends to a flash hotel recently, there were bottles of water on offer for £140 – each! The sort of thing which is designed to take money from people who clearly have too much.

I tell her that when we finish speaking, in about half an hour I will be passing through the 1,000 kms barrier. Then exactly as my Satmap mile counter for today clicks on to 17 kms, 1,000 kms for the trip, my phone buzzes with a text message from Karen congratulating me on it. Exactly, to the second. It is amazing.

Unfortunately, there is nothing of note on the spot, nothing to photograph to mark the occasion. I do think of starting a cairn, but there are no stones available. A bit of a damp squib, really, for such a milestone in VBW

At about 19 kms I find myself walking along quite a wide road, but not particularly busy. Fortunately it has plenty of edge to it – panketo, they call it in Cyprus, that I can walk on. A woman driving past slows down almost to walking pace, toots her horn, waves and smiles. I have had a few of these – I don't know whether there has been something in the papers. This is as I come into St Marceau on the D293.

I toil up the hill into Assé-le-Riboul. A really nice sign saying that it is twinned with Obermorschwihr in Alsace – the sign includes a painting of the Alsatian town.

Gay picks me up in Assé-le-Riboul and takes me to Beaumont-sur-Sarthe, to the campsite, which is the busiest one we have seen. A lot of Brits and Dutch. We go out for a pizza to celebrate the milestone. I have an interesting chat on the campsite with a chap called John. He lives in Milton Keynes but is from Kidsgrove and used to work there for ICL, as I did. We have a few laughs at coincidences which keep coming into the conversation.

Beaumont-sur-Sarthe is obviously schizophrenic as it is also known as Beaumont-le-Vicomte. It is twinned with Burgh le Marsh in Lincolnshire, England.

Total kms for the day were 24, bringing me up to 1,007 kms. Climbs for the day were a meagre 814 metres.

Day 35. Assé-le-Riboul to Sougé-le-Ganelon.

Friday the 18th June. End of the 5th week. Halfway in terms of time.

It's cold, although not as cold as a couple of days ago, when there was a north east wind. Overcast but not raining. In fact it didn't rain yesterday, although it was forecast to do so. It is an ideal temperature for walking.

I seem to have finally got away from cuckoos. I heard some pigeons and was thinking of how boring they sound, which reminded me of cuckoos, which reminded me I have not heard any for several days. This is not a bad thing.

At 7 kms I am climbing up a steep hill into the town of St-Christophe-du-Jambet. It doesn't look a big place but a town with a name like that should have a café, don't you think? The answer is no, which is possibly why nearly all the houses in this village are for sale, or lots more than I have seen anywhere else.

At 15 kms I am coming into Montreuil-le-Chétif. I manage to get a coffee and croissant there. More importantly, a bit of a rest. It must be the smallest bar I have seen in France. A bar/tabac and next door a shop. I assume the whole thing used to be a bar, or a shop and they have made it into two, which is why the bar is so small. Nice croissant, too. I marvel again at how a rest, or possibly the coffee and croissant, can perk you up. I was really flagging until I stopped. Now, I feel amazingly rejuvenated so that the second half of the walk is much friskier than the first half.

I come into Douillet-le-Joly. Reminds me of our next door neighbour and friend Ang Dooley. She is very jolly. In Doullet-le-Joly there is a bar, or rather a building which said Bar on it, but absolutely no sign of activity or commerce – or life. But there is a very interesting garden, with a stuffed birdwatcher peeping out of the hedge.

The garden is also replete with bears, horses and other large ornaments. I have noticed during the past 35 days that the French are very fond of filling their gardens with fake animals, geese, ducks, rabbits and other not very wild life – what's that all about? A French friend of ours plants plastic flowers in her garden.

I have a few twinges in my hamstring, which feels a bit ominous. I walk slowly, trying to ease it off. Soon I forget it, so it must have cleared up.

I spoke too soon about the cuckoos. I can hear one in the distance.

I have forgotten to appreciate the flatness of the last few days walking. There have been a few steep climbs in today's walk. Fortunately I am walking on roads most of the time, so the steepness has not been accompanied by loose rocks and twisting turning, one-foot wide gullies full of syrup.

On the last climb of the day I come into the town where my rendezvous with Gay is – a town which rejoices in the wonderful name of Sougé-le-Ganelon.

When I reach Sougé-le-Ganelon (don't you just love these names – it was worth today's walk, just to be able to say I have been to this place), today's terminus, I realise that I have at last lost the koala which Ang and Paul gave me as I left home. A few days ago it lost its boomerang, which did not come back, and now I feel it has leapt from the brim of my hat in Dooley-the-Jolly, probably because it felt it had reached home. Sorry, Ang and Paul. I will now revert to the backup kangaroo key-ring.

Gay drives us off to the campsite in St. Leonard-des-Bois. This area has the name of Alpes-Mancelles, which sounds ominously hilly.

Did I mention yesterday that when I clocked up the 1,000 kms, this was, with my stride of 0.80 of a metre, my 1,250,000th step of VBW? That is 625,000 steps with each foot, including the left, arthritic one, which is increasingly making me aware of all the hard work it is doing.

Today I felt tired while walking. Maybe this was a bit of anti-climax from yesterday – after all, I still have half the walk to do. Or maybe it was just a tired day – I have mentioned before that some days I feel tired, most days I do not. Mark Knopfler put it very well when he wrote "Some days you're the windscreen, some days you're the bug". I know exactly what he meant. I walked 25.5 kms, 1032.5 to date. Climbs of 899 metres.

And that marks the end of the fifth week and the first half of Vic's Big Walk For Pancreatic Cancer UK.

Chapter 12. The Sixth Week.

Day 36. Sougé-le-Ganelon to la Roche-Mabile

9 kms into Saturday's walk. It's wet and it's miserable. I stop in the small town of St-Cénéri-le-Gérei. It is very, very picturesque. A very Cotswold type of town. Despite the fact that it is wet and miserable, there are people wandering around with cameras, snapping away.

This is the first place on the GR36, the so-called M1 of walkers, where I have actually seen any walkers. They aren't walking, you understand, just milling about waiting, I think, for a restaurant/bar to open. All done up in capes and boots. It is about 2 minutes to 10 so some rule is obviously being adhered to in true bureaucratic fashion. I try the bar. A man is sitting at a table, reading the newspaper. He holds his hand up in barrier fashion. Clearly he doesn't want my business. Or maybe the milling-about group is due in here at spot on 10 and he thinks I am one of them. (Gay yesterday asked the man at the campsite why he couldn't let us out before 8 and he said, "Because it is in the rules". And the rule exists because ... ?)

So I go in a bar/tabac which is almost next door. Have a coffee. No croissants. The walkers disappear. I don't know whether they go into the restaurant or whether they actually carry on somewhere and do some walking.

At 20 kms, which is 1215 today because of the late start caused by imprisonment at the campsite, I am coming into St Denis-sur-Sarthon. St. Denis is, as I was reading only yesterday, horridly busy with traffic. A main road goes through it and one has to have one's wits about one.

Today's plod is 26 kms. Total so far is 1058.5. With a name like Alpes-Mancelles, it isn't surprising to find the hills creeping in again after a few days of flatness. Today's climbs total 965 metres which is nothing to my legs battle-hardened by bigger hills in the middle of France.

I noticed in St-Cénéri-le-Gérei that the car number plates had changed, that I was now in département 61, which is Orne, and that I was in Normandy. As I pressed on, I was in département 53, which is Mayenne, and which is back in Pays de la Loire region. By the time I finished the walk in la Roche-Mabile, I was back in Normandy.

Because the nearby campsite is not yet open for the summer (it is the second half of June!), we are camped in Alençon. Alençon is in Orne. It a big town and not very much to our liking. William the Conqueror took exception to it as well. He laid siege to the town. The citizens defied him by hanging animal skins from the walls, in reference to his ancestry as the illegitimate son of Duke Robert and a tanner's daughter. On capturing the town, William had a number of the citizens' hands cut off in revenge. Alençon is also the home of the famous point d'Alençon lace.

Alençon was also the home to what could become a whole dynasty of saints. Marie-Azélie Guérin Martin and Louis Martin were the parents of St. Thérèse of Lisieux. Now they are on the ladder of sainthood themselves. They were the first spouses in the history of the Catholic Church to be proposed for sainthood as a couple, in 2008.

While I have been moaning about the cold and wet summer (although I think I have also made it clear that this has played into my hands by not being too hot), I have also been aware that there has been a catastrophe, weather-wise, in the Var département in Provence. Many people have been killed and thousands are affected badly by floods resulting from horrendous rainfalls. Apparently these have been the worst rains since the early 1800s. To put that in perspective – since before New Zealand was colonised. France gets much more than its share of natural disasters. This is the second one this year, after the storm and floods near the Atlantic coast earlier in the year, which also resulted in many deaths and many more losing homes to which they will never be able to return.

In our time in France there have been two catastrophic flooding incidents in the Aude, where we live. I have already mentioned that days before the turn of the century two hurricanes slammed into France on consecutive days, causing immense damage, an example of which is that 29,000,000 trees were felled. In the winter of 2008/9 another hurricane caused colossal havoc in Northern Spain and Southern France. And so on, and so on.

Day 37. la Roche-Mabile to Boucé

As I set out from la Roche-Mabile it's bloody freezing, but dry. I check the temperature – 8.9 degrees. June 20th.

Had a bit of a disaster last night. When Gay and I were mapping today's course, I put the course into the Satmap and found it would only go so far then ran into a blank area of the map. Of course! We are in Normandy and need a new SD card, the one for Basse-Normandie. I put it in and there are no GRs visible on the screen. No purple lines. I faffed around with it – kept switching on and off and zooming in and out – no way was it going to show the GRs. I checked and all the other cards are 1:25,000. The Normandie one is 1:50,000. Originally Basse-Normandie was supposed to be doubled up on one of the other cards but it wasn't, so they sent me a card just for BN. Surely even the 1:50,000 should show the GRs? Anyway, it meant we had to re-map the route so that I am walking on roads – this card shows only roads. Yet in the next few days, the GR is probably the best option because it becomes quite direct to Ouistreham. What can we do?

I am down a country lane when I hear a car coming along and I pull over to let it go past. It stops. It creeps along behind me and then pulls up alongside me. It contains 3 young men, one of whom says he saw me yesterday in St Denis. They ask me what I am doing, so I tell them about my walk. It is when they stop and get out that I realise they are drunk. What if they are aggressively drunk and all this is preliminary to jumping on me? But they are friendly, shake hands, and drive off.

I am walking mainly on forestry trails – these must be pretty permanent because they are on my map cards as roads. I see little, hear little. Nothing to report. It is still cold, hasn't warmed up much at all. It becomes very windy in the last few kms, when I have an open road ahead of me, the wind from the north again. Vlad is back.

My walk of 25.5 kms finishes in Boucé and brings VBW to 1084 kms so far. Today I have plunged deeper into Normandy and nearer to the coast. 7 more days of walking in France then we take ship for England.

There have been no coffee stops. I have been on my feet all the way, so plodding a bit. Most of today the forestry tracks I was on were very steep – at one time my forward progress was reduced to 1 kph. My upward speed was probably a little above that. I climbed 1109 metres today.

We have checked into by far the grottiest campsite of the whole trip, so far. We are in Vieux Pont because once again there is no campsite nearer to today's finish. I don't think we shall be coming here for our holidays.

If that sounds like a lot of complaining, I should mention the good news, which is that today, so far, it has been dry. And I believe a sunny day is forecast for tomorrow.

And generally all is OK with the world, my world that is. Maybe I shouldn't have said that.

Day 38. Boucé to Putanges-pont-Ecrepin

21st June. Middle of the year, first action of the morning is to switch the heating on – only the second time in this trip. Then, instead of casting clouts and setting off for a brisk walk in the sunshine (and it is sunny today!) wearing nothing but a loincloth and a pair of hippy sandals, I clap on a thermal vest, zip the legs back on to my shorts for the first time in over a month and set forth with teeth chattering. It is 5 degrees! Good grief! This is the longest day of the year. So, even allowing for continental drift, precession of the equinoxes over the ecliptic and the solar cycle, you would think today would at least be warm, if not the warmest day of the year.

Within 5 kms, the rising of the sun in the sky, plus the heat generated by me charging along trying to stop the icicles forming, make me so uncomfortable that I stop, remove everything (well, almost everything) and stow the Helly-Hansen in my rucksack. After stopping in Écouché for the best pain aux raisins of the trip, and a coffee, I am well warm enough. As long as I keep moving – because although it is a sunny day, wherever I am not protected from the wind, it is a bit touch-and-go, warmth-wise.

Écouché sounds as if it means asleep or recumbent. It is "couch", with an e acute at each end. It's a bigger town than the last few we have been in. It seems to be based on a huge quarry. It always amazes me how much equipment there is at a quarry. It isn't just a case of digging it up and putting it in trucks. Always lots of towers and ramps and crushing noises. And this is one big quarry. I wonder how long they have been digging here? I have seen big quarries before but not virtually in town, as this one is.

I had a funny experience this morning when I awoke. It was freezing in the van. It was only 11 degrees in there even after Gay had put the heating on. So we were cowering under the bedclothes. When I opened my eyes, everything was whirling round and round. It was really weird. A bit frightening. I thought does this mean the end of VBW? Maybe even the end of V? And what else does it mean? I just lay there, things kept whirling and whirling and eventually slowed down, then stopped. I was a bit wary about getting out of bed and standing up. I didn't know what was causing it and still don't. Alarming.

I am following the GR36, which isn't on the Satmap card, of course. So I am following the red and white bars on trees, et cetera. I come to a place where there is barbed wire across. At the side is a wooden fence with a big enough gap for humans to go through. So I assume this might possibly be allowable. I crawl through and follow a footpath across several fields, to be confronted by more barbed wire, but this time without the escape hatch. I take off all my bags and baggage and put them on the ground, crawl under the barbed wire, which fortunately has a bit of give in it so I can hold it up as I pass underneath. And then drag my things through. I have lost count of how many times the GRs seem to have changed, presumably because a farmer withdraws his permission.

A bit of a bummer at Ménil-Jean. I have walked about a kilometre north from there towards Putanges-pont-Ecrepin. I come to a sign saying Private property. I decide to take a stab at it and start walking down the lane – as far as I can see on the map, the only property is off to the side of the lane, which itself goes straight through to Putanges. Of course my timing is bad – a car comes down. It stops. I play the innocent and ask can I go through. The man says no. So I have to go south, west, north and then east. This adds several kms to today's walk.

On last night's campsite we were the only guests. At one time we thought this was about to change when we saw a young couple approaching V-Force One. They were probably going to ask us how to contact the gardienne, so that they could bring in their caravan or tent, or whatever. That would have been an interesting experience for them. When Gay arrived in town she read the sign at the campsite, which said contact the bar. She did so, but the woman at the bar knew nothing. She did not even know who the gardienne was. One of the customers said it was somebody who lived in that house over there. And so it went on. Eventually contact was made. But back to the young couple. They were spared all that detective work. Gay was able to answer their question very easily. The question? "Can we hire this vehicle?" Guess the answer.

If we had rented it to them, they could have frozen to death in there, instead of us.

Today's walk was 29 kms. Total to date 1113 kms. It's getting hilly again – ascents 1163 metres. And we are just entering an area called Suisse Normande, the name sounding not unconnected with hilliness.

Day 39. Putanges-pont-Ecrepin to St Philbert-sur-Orne

As I set off from Putanges I notice the inevitable war memorial. This time the poilou is clutching an olive branch as well as his gun. There are several other monuments, so I go over to have a look. One of them is specifically for British soldiers who died "for our freedom". I haven't seen that before, although later in today's walk I see one out on the open road for an American airman, who died in 1944. The monument was not erected until 1999.

I tried to put a route onto the Satmap last night using the GRs, which Gay clearly has on her paper maps. We tried to assume where the GRs were on the Satmap, but it was such a mess that we eventually gave up and went for the Occam's razor option of finding a route totally by road.

I am walking down one of these mercifully quiet roads when I put up a hare. Wow! Can they go!

It's a lovely sunny day, cold, but not as cold as yesterday, to start with, clearly destined to be warm later.

I am taking it a bit slowly today as I have a slight injury in my left knee. For some years I have had a known problem with my right knee – the injury which stopped me running, but have not had a problem with the left one before. I think I know what caused it. The roads have a very sharp camber in the last metre or so at each side. Of course that is where I walk, generally on the left side, facing the approaching traffic. This means that my left leg is constantly striving to be longer than the right (it is best to alternate sides to avoid this problem, but the interests of safety are paramount), like a haggis. Result, misery. The problem came on yesterday as I came down a very steep descent into Putanges-pont-Écrepin. It doesn't bother me a lot while walking and doesn't seem to be any worse than it was when I started out this morning.

I assume there is an exercise I can do to ease it but the trouble is, I don't know which exercise. If you do the wrong one, especially round such a complex joint as the knee, you can make it worse.

I pass a stone marking the boundary between the Orne and Calvados départements of Normandy. Calvados is the last of the many départements that I will walk through in France. It contains Caen and Ouistreham, our ferry port, so this is clear evidence that we are getting somewhere.

When I see the marker, I have just left Ménil-Hermei, where I had hoped to find a café-bar, having been disappointed in Rabondanges. As these are the only two villages I will be passing through today, my hopes are high, and Ménil-Hermei was the bigger of the two. My hopes are even higher when I spot a boulangerie. I go in, order a croissant, and ask if there is a bar. The answer is no. It seems that I will eat my croissant while walking along, and that my legs will not get the rest they are seeking.

But the woman says, "Did you want a coffee? I can make you one." She asks if I take milk and/or sugar, leaves customers waiting in the shop while she goes off to make the coffee. Clearly she doesn't have any cups there, because the coffee comes in one of those glass jars that sometimes contain prefabricated desserts. I ask if there is a seat anywhere in the village. She gets her husband to take a chair outside for me (it is a tiny shop). Then she says the coffee is a gift. How kind is that? I am really knocked out. The price of a coffee will go into our collecting tin for Pancreatic Cancer research, as does the "cost" of any act of kindness like this.

One of the customers is an old man, who came out with his bread, prepared to mount his trail bike, and asks me about my walk. I think I should stop being surprised that somebody I have categorised as "old" is actually younger than me.

We are in a campsite between St Philbert-sur-Orne and Ménil-Hubert-sur-Orne. Today's walk was only 21 kms, with climbs of 788 metres.

No complaints about the weather. It started out a bit cool, but was clearly going to warm up as soon as the sun started to climb. And it did. The flies have been a bit of a nuisance, but they have probably been waiting for months for a bit of warm weather so they could harass a walker, and I just happened to be handy.

Day 40. St Philbert-sur-Orne to Clécy.

I had a very bad connection with the internet yesterday but I managed to post on my blog and send and receive a few e-mails. One of the e-mails was from Alex and Mark. Alex said she had just discovered my blog and how much she enjoyed it. She is from Manchester and Mark is from Blackpool and they live near Pont d'Ouilly, which is 5 kms into my walk this morning. They wanted to know when I would be walking through Pont d'Ouilly and she would buy me a coffee. She would also donate to Pancreatic Cancer UK. So I sent an e-mail back saying this is the only time I am going to be on the Internet today but here is my phone number. Thinking she would ring and make some arrangement, I also said I would be in Pont d'Ouilly this morning.

I didn't hear back but nevertheless I will be going to Pont d'Ouilly as it is the only place I can possibly get a coffee today. It is slightly off course, a slight detour.

It is a bit cool again. Only 12 degrees in the van, but it is limbering up to be a beautiful day.

On the war memorial in Menhil-Hubert there is mention of various civil victims of WW2, including the curé. Also Jean Grain – fusilé par les SS 15 Aout 1944. 19 years old. 3 English or American names on there as well, without saying they were English or American. Just the three names and ranks on a separate plaque. As with many war memorials in the north of France, there are several artillery shells just in case we should get to thinking that war is a bad thing.

I notice there is a boulangerie as well. It is open. I don't notice whether the bar is. It seems a bit early so I walk past. I hope I won't regret that when I get to Pont d'Ouilly, if I find things closed there.

Quite a wide straight road from Menhil-Hubert to Pont d'Ouilly. Not busy, but what traffic there is, is going fast. Plenty of room on the verges, though.

Cuckoos are still with us. I can hear one belting away.

I stop for the planned coffee in Pont d'Ouilly, without having heard from Alex and Mark, but no sooner am I a couple of kms further on, than the phone rings and it is Alex. Have you already been? Have we missed you? Of course they have. I say we will try to arrange something for Clécy later. A decent walk for me but only a few minutes for them in the car.

I have a long and hard climb through some woods on the GR, takes me back a few weeks. Up a very steep and high ridge. The track is all loose stones, gouged out, eroded bits, wet bits, muddy bits. Quite hard work. Also a lot of brambles, several hundred metres where the path goes through brambles growing all over the path. Very tricky. If you go past them too quickly you can find one wound round your legs. I still have scars on my legs as a result of running past brambles 20 years ago.

While I am in the middle of this, the battery on my Satmap gives up, for the same reason that Gay's phone has already packed in today. We had them on charge last night but the switch on the extension bar had accidentally been knocked off so no juice was getting through.

Fortunately, I have some spare dry-cell batteries with me for the Satmap, so I manage to change them over, although it is very difficult, especially with my eyes. The plug for the adaptor is so tiny. I manage to get it going again and it hasn't lost the data – how far I have walked, et cetera.

I come into Clécy, which has cliffs towering over it, as well as a splendid railway viaduct. It is clearly a place of much river activity. Coming into town I have to fight my way through several groups of kids being led off to experience something which involves crash helmets and lifejackets.

The campsite is on the other side of the river, so I have to make quite a detour round to it. Lots of cafes, ice cream places, eateries. It all looks very active, but not too full of people just yet. That will all change as soon as July starts.

Gay has arranged a haircut for me. I just manage to have a shower, lunch, and the haircut before we meet Alex, Mark, daughter Cassie and springer spaniel Max. We meet in town but walk down to one of the river cafes for a coffee and then move to another for an ice cream. We spent a very pleasant afternoon down there.

I have now spent 40 days and 40 nights wandering in the wilderness, and am wondering when the wisdom and wonderful insights will arrive. Maybe, because of inflation, I will have to wait until I have completed the full 70. One month tomorrow.

It was a short walk today, only 17.5 kms, although some of it was rather testing. This is where Gay's savagery with the navigational axe is paying off. And a day off which had crept into the schedule unannounced has also been sacrificed. We decided it was best to keep moving and to shorten some of the other days instead. I have walked 1151.5 kms since leaving home and there will be five more walking days until we hit the ferry on Sunday.

It has been another sunny day. I think that makes three on the trot. It's a bit unnerving. Our friend Rod in Reading tells us that southern England is desperately in need of rain. Don't worry, Rod, I'm sure we can fix that.

As I mentioned before, one of the things I have noticed almost daily while walking through France is the severe lack of places to sit and rest awhile.

In New Zealand they have an organisation, originally founded, I think, by a lady called Plunket. This organisation provides, all over the country, Plunket Rooms for women and children, safe havens where they can do womanly and childrenly things, undisturbed by the brute male of the species.

I propose to start a similar organisation in France. I am looking for a man called Plonk-It, ideally Lord or Marquis Plonk-It, who will act as patron and figurehead of the Plonk-It Society. But don't you worry, Lord Plonk-It, wherever you are – I will do all the work. The objective of the Plonk-It Society will be simple. It will provide, at every country crossroad in France, and down every country lane, a seat where weary walkers can Plonk their best features, henceforth to be known as It, while they chew the cud, slurp their water, and generally give their legs, and It, a wee rest.

This idea is the culmination of almost 70 years of education, experience, thought and consideration. It is my masterwork.

Today I saw a very rare example of the very few existing Plonk-It facilities, and the only one I have ever seen with full sun protection. I have photographed it and will get my designers to use it as the basis of a prototype.

Day 41. Clécy to Thury-Harcourt.

I walk through a place called Nid de Chien. Dog's Nest. What's the story behind that? This area – Suisse Normande – is a bit of a revelation. I think we are not the only ones to be surprised to find such a hilly area this far north in France, not far from the Channel. The river Orne meanders famously, and as a result, so do the roads and tracks. This river and its ancestors have carved their way down through the rock for hundreds of millions of years to create this spectacular landscape. The cliffs which loom over Clécy are the oldest exposed rocks on the planet. They find fossils here that otherwise we would not wot of.

I experience some of the result of all this carving this morning. Almost straight out of the campsite I am confronted with a very steep road. Fortunately, because like most roads, it twists and turns, I can not see the whole of it or I may have fainted on the spot. The climb, on this one road, is about 250 metres. At the top I am fairly steaming. When I set off it was cool, so I donned one of my excellent Columbia lightweight waterproof jackets. At the top of the hill I have to remove this because it is clinging wetly to me.

I am then walking along a ridge high above the long views of countryside which I can see in every direction.

Today's walk to Thury-Harcourt is short and I arrive in the town before Gay, who is delayed by the haircut she had booked for 9 am in Clécy (I had one yesterday). Because I know she is not yet at the campsite, I install myself at one of the many bars in Thury and proceed to consume coffee until she turns up.

The campsite is quiet but reasonably busy. As is frequently the case, almost everybody else here is Dutch – they do like their caravanning, and their hilly areas, possibly because a speed bump would count as a mountain in their own country.

I covered 17 kms today, the shortest walk of the trip so far. I am enjoying these short ones in the knowledge that when we hit England on Monday, I will be straight into a week of 30 kms days. Distance to date is 1168.5 kms, climbs today 855 metres.

Day 42. Thury-Harcourt to Mutrécy.

Totally on GRs today, which is interesting because, as you know, the SD card Satmap have given me for Normandy does not show GRs. So it's up to the maps to know where I should be, the Satmap to know where I am and, hopefully, waymarkers so that I won't need to resort to the maps very much because, at the risk of being boring, I can't read them very well.

It's a bit up and down. The first 3 kms takes me an hour. Some steep climbs with awkward paths, steep laterally as well as upwards. I pass through woods where there are trees fallen across the path and generally blocking it. At about 3 kms I am walking close to a fence and see a fox shoot away on the other side. It is about two feet away from me when it starts to go. Obviously the fox sees me before I see it. I don't see it until it moves – I always walk along with my eyes glued to the track, especially when it is uneven.

I think this is a day when I won't have a coffee stop. I don't seem to be going through anywhere of reasonable size. I see another fox in the woods, but this one is well dead, not much of it left.

I come to Brieux where I need to turn right. This is after 8 kms but because of the terrain it has taken me over 2 hours of walking. More in hope than expectation, I ask a man if there is a bar or café in the village. No, he says, not for a long way. I thank him and walk on. He calls me back. There is a hotel where you could get a coffee. Is it far, I ask. Nobbut a cockstride, he says. Actually, he says about half a kilometre. This is a diversion, you understand, not on the route. So I walk to the Auberge du Pont, as indicated. Door open, young blonde sweeping up outside. Are you open, says I. No, she says, not until midday. I was just after a coffee, I says. We don't open the doors until 11.30, she says. What a difference from the woman in the boulangerie who went to so much trouble to coffee me up the other day at Ménil-Hermei. So I toil back to Brieux, not trying to think about the wasted time and distance.

I walk through the Foret de Grimbosq. I have heard dreadful things about it being a dead forest of just pine trees, no life. The bit I am walking through is all deciduous and I can hear lots of birds. But I am not actually on the GR 36. I seem to have mislaid that somewhere, so I am walking on the road, which goes directly to Mutrecy.

I was saying some time ago that I was having a lot of trouble with the arthritic joint on my left foot and I thought it was because of the constant walking. But I haven't had any trouble for a while. Or maybe I have just got used to it.

My walk to Mutrécy is only 16 kms but some of the walk is quite testing. All hard work, especially in the hot weather which has suddenly come among us.

So, 1184.5 kms so far. Just 772 metres of climb today.

Six weeks walking under my belt, or rather, under my soles

We are getting very close to the coast. Tomorrow's walk will finish on the outskirts of Caen. Sunday's walk, during which, for the first time, I will have company, will take us directly to the ferry port.

I am looking forward to walking with Dale, even though I have not met him before, but if I had played my cards wrong, I could have had a walking companion for the whole of VBW. In the early days of planning and preparation, I heard from a chap in Spain. I will suppress his name because I don't think one should mock the afflicted in public.

He said that he would like to walk with me all the way, if only I would start in Spain. Spanish TV and press were very interested. I thought this was a bit odd because my walk is clearly intended to have a number of symbolic points, one of which is that it is from my current abode to the house of my birth – a retracing of the steps of my life, back to its beginning. Starting somewhere else would rather spoil that. Not to mention that it would also make the walk impossible to complete in 70 days, thereby removing another piece of symbolism.

This same man at one point asked me for the registered charity number of Pancreatic Cancer UK, so that his company could make a donation. When I asked him, a few weeks later, if there was any progress with the donation which he had suggested, he rounded on me with an angry e-mail. How dare I ask what he, a man of the cloth, gives to charity? Such things are confidential! Et cetera! Et cetera! I breathed a sigh of relief – if I had been daft enough to accept his initial offer, I could have been spending months in the company of a madman.

Chapter 13. The Seventh Week

Day 43. Mutrécy to Fleury-sur-Orne.

Saturday. We spent another night in Thury-Harcourt last night because there doesn't seem to be another campsite between there and the other side of Caen.

As I set off from Mutrécy there are no signs at the turn for the GR. Fortunately Gay pointed the junction out to me when she came to pick me up yesterday. It's another fine day. That must be almost a week of fine weather now. I have actually been very lucky with the weather on this trip. When I was walking in May and June last year it was very hot and humid. I wasn't looking forward to that for 70 days this year. I certainly haven't had it for most of the trip.

It's a very quiet walk, with little of note to report. In Clinchamps-sur-Orne I find another village with a boulangerie but no café-bar, or rather there is one but it is not active. I eat my bun on the run.

I am nearly at the end of the French section. Just 22 kms to do tomorrow. Am I really going to get to the ferry without seeing another walker? Once again this spell seems about to be broken when I spy a man walking towards me, but as before it doesn't count because he is carrying nothing and is clearly just out for a local stroll.

It is the first day of the seventh week of VBW. I have walked for 43 days without a rest, although today is the shortest walk so far. 13 kms – I should have walked a further 2.5 to bring the total so far to 1200 exactly. As it happens, the total is 1197.5 kms. Tomorrow's 22 kms should bring the sum for the French leg to not much over 1200 – the estimate when we set out was 1300 – Gay's navigation has chopped it down.

So much so that we are just dallying around because we are ahead of schedule. By maintaining a normal daily distance we could have caught the ferry a couple of days ago, but this would have made a mess of all sorts of arrangements in England.

We fetch up on the edge of Fleury-sur-Orne. For the first time in weeks, I end up with dusty legs. That's because it is the first time in weeks that I have walked somewhere with really dry ground.

There is no campsite available. We head off to spend the evening in a layby outside the house of a new friend we made as a result of him making a donation to Pancreatic Cancer UK through my blog. Dale and Thérèse have also invited us for an evening meal. And tomorrow Dale will be walking with me the very last section of the French segment of VBW.

Ascents scaled down today to a measly 422 metres.

Day 44. Fleury-sur-Orne to Ouistreham.

Dale and I head off on a route which takes us from Fleury-sur-Orne, straight through the centre of Caen to Ouistreham.

Next to the yacht basin in Caen there is a large market in full swing. Gay would have liked to see that, but she has moved V-Force One to Ouistreham by this time. Dale and I do not miss the opportunity to sample one of the many cafés bordering the market square.

From Caen, we follow the wide ship canal. The track is awash with cyclists, roller-bladers and runners. One could almost think one was in California. In this country which has so many cyclists, I have been amazed by how few I have seen in the last 6+weeks. I certainly make up for that today. I just wish cyclists would learn to sound some sort of audible alarm before they sweep past pedestrians.

A ship comes past us – a rare sight on this canal these days, although probably not as rare as on the Manchester Ship Canal, which I should see on my travels, and which, as a lad, I used in earnest when I was a Radio Officer on the good ship Manchester Spinner.

We pause again at Pegasus Bridge, a bascule bridge which crosses the Canal. It was a major objective of Operation Tonga, in the opening minutes of the invasion of Normandy during World War II. A glider-borne unit of the British was to land, take the bridges intact and hold them until relieved. The successful taking of the bridges played an important role in limiting the effectiveness of a German counter-attack in the days and weeks following the invasion.

In 1944 it was renamed Pegasus Bridge in honour of the operation. The name is derived from the shoulder emblem worn by the British airborne forces, which depicts the flying horse Pegasus.

The house near Pegasus Bridge was the first to be liberated during D-Day. It still exists and today contains a café and a small museum shop that sells Pegasus Bridge related material. Arlette Gondrée, who now runs Café Gondrée, was a small child living in the home when it was liberated. It is at this café that Dale and I partake of tea and perchance a small croissant.

We reach the lighthouse in Ouistreham, which indicates the end of the road for Vic's Big Walk in France. It is almost next to the ferry quay where this evening we shall take ship for England and 26 more days of walking.

We have lunch with Thérèse and Dale (not forgetting Enzo, their grandson), with whom we also shared an excellent dinner yesterday evening. I thank Dale for his company during today's walk. I look forward to meeting some of his friends, the Walters, as I transit from Cheshire to Lancashire in a few weeks time.

Now it is on to Portsmouth via the overnight ferry and the start of my journey through Britain. It was 1968 when I first read Journey Through Britain, John Hillaby's famous account of his epic walk. He had made the journey the year before, at the age of 50.

The book is memorable for me in a number of ways. It was the first of many volumes which I have read over the years about prolific walkers. When I was searching for the book recently, to refresh my memory and to see if I could glean any useful tips from it, I had a very clear picture in my mind of the delightful book cover, with its picture of a blue tit perched on a pair of walking shoes.

Another thing about the book is that it demonstrates to the user that it is not written by a superman. Hillaby frequently expresses doubts about his ability to go on. He gets miserable and hates what he is doing. He is not above admitting that the offer of a lift can be tempting. Even on the first day, a few hours after setting off from Land's End, he is overcome by weariness and has a 20 minute kip before he can carry on.

He carries a tent and gear for any accidental self-sufficiency, but is always very pleased to come across a hotel at the end of the day. Just as well – on his very first night, camping in St Ives, he is moved on by the police. It is no fun being a vagrant in Britain.

After a few days his calf muscles go on strike and he thinks the walk has come to an end. The hotel porter, "an ex-professional in the boxing game" is called in for a consultation. He recommends exercise. A reporter comes looking for the person walking to John o' Groats, just as Hillaby hobbles out of a lift with a stick.

He gets going again, and re-discovers those days when the walking becomes effortless and almost sublime, somewhat like the so-called "runners' high".

How the world has changed since 1967. At a launderette in Stoke, he thinks it worth remarking that a young woman is washing, among other things, a man's shirt and underwear – and yet she is not wearing a wedding ring! Oh, shame and scandal in de family!

Of course, he meets interesting people and sees fascinating places. It is a book worth reading, but, as I planned my own walk, I was re-reading books like this on the lookout for tips. Hillaby has several for me. One is to plan the route well, especially in the matter of avoiding traffic – British drivers are not noted for giving pedestrians a wide berth. Another is, yet again, to drink plenty. A key factor when walking long distance, one which I believe I already have covered, is to be very careful in the choice of footwear. Hillaby went to great pains to find shoes which were more flexible and supple than the army-style clompers which hikers of the period normally used, and yet he had foot problems. In fact he lost most, possibly all, of his toenails. Amazingly, one pair of shoes lasted the whole trip, but only just – the soles were falling off near the end and he had to sew them on again.

Day 45. Portsmouth to Kilmeston.

Septimus meets me off the ship at Portsmouth so that he can walk the first two English sections with me. What a day he picked!
First we go to the hotel where Mr and Mrs Septimus stayed last night. This is a Travelodge. We were going to have coffee – in fact I had asked him to find a Costa but they were all in the wrong direction from our setting-off point. At the hotel, the choice was coffee from an urn, or tea which you had to make yourself, with hot water from an urn. Welcome to Britain.
It is very hot – 30 degrees I learn later. The estimate for Portsmouth to Kilmeston is 30 kms. We walk almost due north through the streets of Portsmouth.
Portsmouth is initially flat but surprisingly hilly once we cross the A27. At one point Paul (the alias of Septimus) is trying to check we are on the right road – as usual there are no street names visible. He crosses the road to speak to a woman at a bus stop. He waves me across, saying it is the right direction. When I go over the woman is saying well done, et cetera. Clearly, Septimus has told her about VBW. I tell her that I am doing it to raise funds for Pancreatic Cancer UK. She gives me a five pound note.
We join the Wayfarers Walk, on which we are to stay for the rest of the day. This route, like many long distance footpaths, swings east and west, in some cases heads south again, and we had found the distance difficult to estimate. I think I have mentioned that we have one of those electronic gadgets which you run over the map and which comes up with the answer. It is hopeless. I now loathe this device. I will despise it even more by the end of the day.
The 30 kms eventually turn out to be 43 kms. It is dreadful. It is a really hot day, at least 30 degrees in the shade, which is in rather short supply.
There is little sign of anywhere to have a break. We cross a golf course at one point. There are two men looking for a lost ball. I find the ball, then I find another one on the path. I take the opportunity, while giving the balls to this man, to proselytise. I get the impression he may donate and some weeks later he does so. He signs himself on the JustGiving website "The Golfer".
We are gagging for a drink and just coming up to some habitation. I ask a man who is sweeping outside the golf club if there is a café in town. He says yes, in here. I am a bit surprised because I have the impression that golf clubs like to keep non-members out. It is very nice, we have coffee, a glass of water and some cake which looks like that stuff they sell in some French bakeries and call Pudding. It is very heavy and stodgy. Excellent. Probably fuels us a bit for the rest of the arduous day.
Off we go, up the track. We haven't gone far before we are confronted by private enterprise, in the shape of a large gentleman sitting on one of those electric buggies which keep disabled people mobile. At first we think he may be the lone survivor from

a Zulu ambush because there are spears and assegais sticking out in all directions. But no, he himself is the ambusher, lying in wait for weary walkers and trying to sell them one of the many walking sticks and poles he carries with him. We politely decline, hand him our calling card, and trudge on. I bought a pair of walking poles before starting the trek, but have not used them once. My hands are too full with navigation devices, cameras, dictation equipment and water bottles.

We pass through few habitations, which to me represent the possibility of another coffee stop. We come down a long, narrow lane and find ourselves in Hambledon.

Hambledon is known as the Cradle of Cricket. The Hambledon Cricket Club is thought to have been founded in about 1750. There is even a pub here called the Bat and Ball. This is mildly amusing because Pat and Paul often sign their e-mails Bat and Ball.

We enquire of a lady whether there is a café in town. She says yes but it is closed because it is Monday but I will take you home for a cup of tea. She then drives us in her BMW back up the lanes down which Septimus and I have just walked. She produces a full lunch on the farmhouse table. I am not hungry and restrict myself to the cup of tea. Septimus is slightly less restrained. He is also a bit trepidatious that we shall have to cover the same ground by walking down the lane again. But the lady, whose name we never discover, drives us back to the spot where she had found us. Her husband hadn't turned a hair at two waifs and strays being brought into the house. In response to a query from Septimus, he tells us, "Aye, she brings all sorts home."

The walk drags on and on. The trail is very up and down, overgrown in many places, badly signed in others, nonexistent at a couple of points. At one stage the track crosses a very large field. At the entrance to the field is a sign warning of bulls. The field is so big, and the track across it so steep, that if a bull approaches us in the middle, we will be completely helpless. Fortunately, all bovine life-forms are cowering from the heat in the shade of a wood at the edge of the field.

Eventually we arrive at the rendezvous point in Kilmeston after six in the evening. This is the longest walk I have ever done. We have walked 43 kms, longer than a marathon. We have been on the go for 12 hours. Although there were no big climbs, the total of the many minor climbs was 1861 metres, over 6,000 feet and the most of any day during VBW. We have been on the Wayfarer's Walk all day but, although we met and talked to several people, all of them kind and friendly, we did not see another walker.

The distance measurer is so unreliable, the estimate so far from reality, that we now have to completely replan and reschedule all the walking between here and Oxford. It was easier to estimate in France because we were using larger scale maps. Also it will be easy to estimate distance for the canal walking from Oxford onwards. We shall be arriving in Reading one day late. I suspect that for the rest of the trip we will be two days behind. There is plenty of slack later in the walk, but the rescheduling could affect all the arrangements we have made for people to meet us and walk with me for a stage or so.

Day 46. Kilmeston to Brown Candover.

After yesterday's immense walk, I tried to activate the UK dongle which I bought in March especially for this purpose. I had carefully explained at PC World why I needed it, the project I was undertaking, that I would not be wanting to activate it until June, and that I did not live in the UK. I was assured that the dongle package from "3" was fully fit for this purpose.

When I got home (still in March) and examined the package, I saw that I had to activate it within 13 days, and that I could not use it unless I had a UK address. Before setting off on VBW I spent many a long hour trying to sort this out with both PC World and "3" (the latter being in India, of course, and completely unable to understand my problem). I was assured from all sides that, whatever it said on the tin, it would work for me. Of course yesterday, crunch time, I was told that, unless I had a UK address which was linked to my bank account (and of course I do not, as I had explained many times, because I live in France) the package which I have bought and paid for will not work.

This left me up the creek without a dongle. As it happens, there was a Holiday Inn next to last night's campsite, where Mr and Mrs Septimus were staying. I was able to go there, buy a drink, and use their WiFi. In the evening, Bat and Ball invited us to the hotel for a good meal.

When we examined the maps in light of yesterday's experience, it was clear that today we were heading for another walk of 40+ kms so we shortened it and planned to walk from Kilmeston to Brown Candover.

A very nice lady called Abby in Cheriton tells us that, although there is no café in the village, there are lots in Alresford, that we should go to Tiffins, and say she sent us.

Alresford has a definite Saxon ring to it, at least to the untutored ears of Septimus and me. There appears to be no record of Saxon activity in this area, but as we are walking through extensive dense woodland somewhere between Cheriton and Alresford, we come upon an encampment which has all the appearance of being there since historical times.

The defenders have cunningly placed a green woodpecker to distract us. It works. But then we spot some decidedly dodgy caravans lurking in the woods. They are very much the worse for wear. One of them is painted overall in red – as Aztec pyramids were, after a heavy sacrifice session – is something similar going on here? There is a pervading air of menace.

There are various bits of heavy equipment scattered along a stretch of about a third of a mile. Have the Saxons/Aztecs been getting together with the Dukes of Hazard or Steptoe and Son? Sep remarks that it puts him in mind of the film "Deliverance" and Duelling Banjos. Having led a more sheltered life, I am not familiar with this and can neither agree nor disagree, but it all looks distinctly shady.

The path narrows and after a while we see a four-wheel drive car approaching followed by a large dog. The car occupies almost the full width of the track and we have to squeeze past.

The occupants look like pirates, smugglers, drug dealers or slave traders. The overall impression is all of missing teeth, Satanic visage, leering looks and evil. We feel they are obviously weighing us up as victims. Septimus determines that if a door opens he will ask no questions before rendering the opener unconscious; he trains with a professional so that he can do these things.

The pirates/Saxons/Aztecs/Dukes/Steptoes – by now probably totally confused about their identities – I certainly am – think better of it and carry on slowly. We are somewhat relieved to reach Alresford and civilisation.

This makes such an impression on Septimus that months later he tells me that if we had disappeared in that forest they would still be looking for us and that it was a good job I was not alone.

As Septimus and I are walking through the streets of Alresford in search of Tiffins, we espy a walker, rucksack, maps and all. He set out from Winchester yesterday, on his first multi-day walk, to follow the Pilgrims' Way. He intends to average 10 kms or miles a day, his companion has already deserted after one day, and he has just found out that the Pilgrims' Way goes to Mont St Michel in France, not just to Canterbury. I don't know whether this is true or not, but he seems pretty alarmed at the idea. In 1,300 kms of walking, in France and England, on major trails, this was one of very few walkers I have seen.

At Tiffins we have a splendid time talking to some people who inform us that Alresford is the centre of the watercress industry in Britain, and that there is a private railway line, with several steam engines (we have just seen one), just to take the watercress to market.

On Abbotstone Common we meet Philip Russell, along with his wife and daughter and a Rhodesian Ridgeback dog. Philip says, "Hey, I'm 70 next year! I'll join you then". I remind him that I am doing my walk now and hope to have finished before next year. Later, he makes a contribution online.

We march on to Brown Candover, but not before I have startled Septimus by bursting into song, to demonstrate a radio advert we are talking about.

My beer's a Rheingold, a dry beer
Think of Rheingold whenever you buy beer
It's not bitter, not sweet

It's an extra dry treat
Think of Rheingold whenever you buy
Even though I have never been a beer drinker, I remember this song from 1957 or 1958, the last time I was in New York. It is almost as long as that since anybody heard me sing. I surprise myself more than Septimus, who comments on the fine quality of my baritone voice. I believe he is flattering me in the hope of getting me to return to the singing fold. We come from a singing family and I have no idea why or when I stopped, but I have not let rip in song for at least 30 years. Maybe this walk is changing me in some way?

Today we walked a mere 22.5 kms, giving us an average for the two days of well over 30 kms, and a total to date of 1285. Today's climbs were 919 metres.

Day 47. Brown Candover to Sherborne St. John.

Wednesday. Septimus went home yesterday, straight from the finish of the day's walk in Brown Candover. Gay drops me back in Brown Candover this morning so that I can walk to north of Basingstoke. The Wayfarers Walk is hardly used, it is so overgrown. I toil through nettles up to my armpits.

It is very humid today, as it has been for a few days. On today's map there are lots of disused pits. I am wondering what type of pit, when I discover the answer. Written on a log is "Free chalk". I check and, sure enough, the pits, which are more like small quarries, have visible chalk.

I reach Dummer. I remember this was in the news when the Hon. Sarah Ferguson was about to become the Duchess of Pork. I am hoping with that sort of association it will be a tourist trap, replete with cafes.

In the village I ask a group of young mothers, who are placing their offspring on the school bus, if there is a café nearby. Nothing doing, but we have a bit of a conversation about VBW. One of the ladies has lost her mother to pancreatic cancer and later donates via my JustGiving page.

The ladies have told me that as I cross the motorway there will be a Sainsburys supermarket, which has either a Costa or a Starbucks. I cross the motorway but see no sign of a supermarket of any description.

Later as I am passing Basingstoke on an incredibly straight road which clearly once belonged to the Romans, another lady with a bike asks me if I have seen much. I suppose maybe, having seen all the equipment dangling from me, she thinks I am a bird-watcher. Of course, in 1,300 kms I have seen much, so we talk about that for a while.

I march on to Sherborne St John. Gay has told me she is parked at a pub, but I can't find it. I just can not find any way to get north of the church. Eventually a kind gentleman puts me right. The pub is to the south of the church and I have already passed it. VF-1 is parked in a quiet corner so after I shower we go into the pub for our wedding anniversary lunch.

Then we plunge into Basingstoke in search of a PC World, where we change the dongle for one which can actually do the business.

Another short day of 21 kms. 1306 kms to date.

Day 48. Sherborne St. John to Caversham, Reading.

For the second half of the walk on Monday I had a pain in my kidney area, which reminded me very much of the incident when I spent all day in hospital in Christchurch, NZ. On that occasion, despite being tested in all sorts of ways, including a CT-scan, they found nothing but decided I must have had a kidney stone and passed it before the testing commenced. This time it didn't become severe, as it did in NZ. I still have it, a few days later, but less so. Maybe I am not going to end the walk in hospital instead of in Blackpool.

The track I am on now is more of the same Wayfarers Walk. It's like a bloody jungle. The nettles are higher than my shoulders, they meet in the middle of the track. Brambles growing over the track, long grass. It really shows very little sign of use, never mind maintenance.

The campsite we were in last night was a goodly drive from Sherborne St John, where I finished yesterday's walk and had to start today's. When we booked in, the proprietor gave Gay half the money back to go into the fund. It is now in the purple container and will eventually find its way onto my JustGiving webpage. The pitch next to us was still empty when we went to bed, although clearly occupied, as we could tell by a few chairs which were arranged as strategically as German towels. When we awoke this morning, it was obvious that the wanderers had returned while we were unconscious. It was also apparent that they had parked the front wheel of their Kon-Tiki on top of our electricity cable. So they had to be knocked up, if you will pardon the expression. We expected aggression but received only contrition – "It was dark when we returned" – so there were no on-the-spot executions.

It is all roads today – the only time, I think, that this will happen in England, for which I am very grateful. The first third is pretty quiet. The next third is a bit frightening – driving in England is much faster and more aggressive, which doesn't go down too well with a pedestrian on roads with no pavement and with hedges which meet the road, leaving nowhere to go, and with lots of blind bends.

The last third is pretty horrifying. I used to be very familiar with Reading, and it has been a building site for 40 years, in my experience. But the remoulding of the vehicle-bearing landscape at the M4 junction exceeds everything I have seen before. It is probably very alarming for a motorist to navigate it, but you ain't seen nothing unless you try to get past it as a pedestrian. But it is very nice of the hard-hat man, when I ask him how he would negotiate it, to say he would round up some of the guys and make a donation. Unfortunately, this does not come to pass.

As I pass along one of the main streets of Reading, a young man tells me that my taser-like device is regarded as a Class 3 firearm in Britain. I don't know how true this is but decide that I had better cease carrying it with me.

It is very generous of a man at Reading Bridge, when I ask him which direction I should take on the towpath to Caversham Bridge, to dive into his pocket to make a donation on the spot. I give him a card and say that, if he still wants to make a donation when I am not looming over him, he can do it online.

It is strange to find myself outside Reading Bridge House. The company I worked for long ago was based there and I had to visit that building at least once a month, frequently more often. But I have not been to the building for 30 years. Rod and Caroline, with whom we are staying for the next two nights, both worked at Reading Bridge House in the olden days.

I walk along to Caversham Bridge, where Gay comes to pick me up. She has already checked in with Rod and Caroline, but they are both out for a while. We have lunch at Costa then drive to the house. Because of the cock-up on the estimation front, we are re-configuring the rest of the trip. We have arrived in Reading a day later than planned. By the time we are on the canal network, we shall be two days behind schedule.

Day 49. Caversham to South Stoke.

More nostalgia today, and of course there will be more and more as I travel through parts of England where I have spent some of my life.

I walked down to Caversham Bridge. Here I used to stay regularly at the eponymous hotel, which was one of character. It has now been knocked down and replaced by a modern Crowne Plaza establishment. Where I used to go for a run of a morning, along the Thames towpath, there is now, for some distance, a tarmac path. There is a huge number of swans and geese in the area, which seem determined to obliterate said path with their waste products. I chat to a Sikh man tossing bread to about 50 swans and more geese. As was the case 30 years ago, there are scullers skimming up and down the Thames, many of them practising, no doubt, for Henley Regatta, which is due to start imminently. I was taught to row, on the Thames, by a former Henley champion, and have always enjoyed that feeling of surging through the water. I would love to do it daily, but have never lived near enough to a body of water. I make frequent use of a Concept 2 trainer, though.

Several people are inclined to talk, or ask me what I am up to. One man says that he makes film documentaries about extraordinary people. He is interested in interviewing me for a film.

Where the path rejoins the river at Purley, there is a lock, with a Locks Café. I stop for a cup of tea, served by a man with zero customer interface skills. Another customer asks me if I am going far, so of course I tell him. In conversation with him and his wife, who have just canoed from Oxford, it turns out that he was once a personnel officer in ICL, the company I worked for in the 70s.

I pass a field, containing not only a football pitch and a children's playground, but also a group of weight-training machines. Do they not rust?

The Thames path is surprisingly hilly in parts, where it swings away from the river, at Purley and Pangbourne for instance. Apparently I pass George Michael's house at Goring, and after Rod, Caroline and Gay pick me up at South Stoke, we see Billy Connolly walking along the street, also in Goring. Who said this is a celebrity-free walk?

Distance covered was 24 kms, 1358 to date, with a surprising total of ascents at 852 metres.

Chapter 14. The Eighth Week.

Day 50. South Stoke to Abingdon.

Yesterday afternoon I received a message that Radio Berkshire wanted my telephone number because they wanted to interview me before I entered Oxfordshire. As Oxfordshire starts about 3 inches from Caversham, I had already plunged well out of Berkshire, in yesterday's walk. But as I was back in Berkshire for the evening, and as we were only 500 metres from Radio Berkshire, I released the secret details of my number, but did not hear from them. And I must say that I know they had the number more than a week ago because Rod King sent it to them, and many other media outlets in the area.

Last evening we had a very pleasant meal out at the Kyrenia Cypriot restaurant in Caversham, with our hosts Caroline and Rod. At the restaurant we met for the first time, and dined with, Sue Ballard, the founder of Pancreatic Cancer UK, who has been a great supporter of my walk.

Back to South Stoke this morning for the start of the walk to Abingdon. It is apparent from the start that it is going to be a hot day. Lots of boats on the River Thames. I thought boating was supposed to be a quiet holiday? This lot are falling over each other.

I have to leave the river at Wallingford. The route is going to take me through the town, so I ask a woman, just before I leave the towpath, if there will be a café. "Oh, no," she says, as if to say, "Nothing so common". I remember once, a woman in a fish and chip shop in Alderley Edge, when asked if they had mushy peas, said, "Oh no" in just such a fashion. She added, "This is Alderley Edge, you know!" They went out of business soon after. But back to Wallingford, I find that there are several cafes, some of them available, and even some of the pubs seem to be open. It is before 9 am.

I stop at the Barley Mow, in Clifton Hampden, for a desperately needed tea or coffee. The time is about 11.30 and they are not due to open until 12.00. The kind mine host gives me a glass of water.

As I charge on along the Thames Path, I overtake a woman who is doing something with her rucksack. She says, "Are you the man who is walking to Blackpool?" Fame at last! Or not. It seems that before Clifton Hampden, she had spoken to somebody going the other way, who had previously spoken to me. Then she had overtaken me while I was having the glass of water. She is walking the Thames Path from the Thames Barrier to the source, doing it in stages on different weekends.

A bit further up the track we meet a young woman going the other way, who asks, "Is it far to Abingdon?" So we turn her around and the three of us proceed in convoy to Abingdon. At one point the younger woman, who is an expert on aquifers, but not, it seems, on keeping herself hydrated, says she will have to have a rest because of the heat. I walk on with the other lady, then I worry about whether I should have left the young one alone, if she will be OK, should we have stayed with her.

When I arrive at Abingdon, Gay promptly drives me back to Clifton Hampden, where it seems we are to be ensconced in a caravan park, which I have already seen, next to the aforementioned Barley Mow, which I believe is the pub which featured in the classic book "Three Men and a Boat".

Day 51. Abingdon to Pear Tree Roundabout, nr Oxford.

Back to Abingdon this morning for the last bit of the Thames Path, as far as I am concerned. The beginning of the Oxford Canal is very close to the Thames, so it would have been an easy transition. Instead I chose to walk into the heart of Oxford, not having been there for many a long year.

On my way in I pass the Iffley Road running track where Roger Bannister, ably assisted by Chris Brasher and Chris Chataway, was the first person to run a mile in less than 4 minutes, in 1954. There is a sign to draw your attention to all this, but it is hung on a sad-looking corrugated iron fence.

Marshals are poised to close off some of the roads in Oxford because it seems a carnival is due to pass this way. I manage to get over a road, into a café, to feed and water my face, get back over the road and on my way before the road is closed.

On my way out of Oxford, I pass the Randolph Hotel and can not even remember why it was I used to stay there. I follow the OS map, in Satmap form, back to the canal, only to find that the street from which I expected to debouch onto the canal bank is in fact a dead end. I return to a street which runs parallel with the canal, but which has many smaller streets heading in the direction of the non-running water (my late friend Richard Burman frequently asked people if they could "point him in the direction of running water" – he used this phrase as other people would refer to "spending a penny"). Any or all of these streets could be dead ends. Fortunately, I espy a couple coming out of their house and ask for help. Not only do they show me the way to go, but they insist on crossing my palms with silver intended for the purple Pancreatic Cancer UK collecting tin which we keep in V-Force One.

The canal is very crowded with boats, mainly parked, including some with alarming jungles growing all over their roofs. I am very surprised by all the apartment blocks built right up to the canal bank on the other side. They go on for quite some distance.

I have arranged to meet Gay at the Pear Tree Roundabout Services. She texts to tell me the service area is closed for refurbishment but she is taking tea at the Holiday Inn next door. It seems to me, when I am close, that the whole area is being refurbished. Lots of roadworks, which have resulted in closure of the canal towpath. I come up onto a very busy road and, in order to make my way to the Holiday Inn, have to cross building sites, climb fences, force my way through one of those impenetrable thickets they build on the slopes of motorways and other fast roads, and inch my way along one of these fast roads, on the inside of the crash barrier, which is frequently being assaulted, as am I, by the thicket. I eventually make my way to the Holiday Inn, with skin battered, bruised and torn.

Judging by the difficulty we then have driving off the Holiday Inn car park onto Pear Tree Roundabout on a Sunday, it will be very unpleasant for Gay after she has dropped me off there tomorrow morning.

We are housed on another Caravan Club CL site, which means that we are camped in a field, with very few facilities. There is a water tap. Nothing else. And we are locked in here until 8 am tomorrow morning.

I walked 24.5 kms. VBW total 1413.5 kms. Today was far too hot for walking. Have England and France swapped weather systems?

Day 52. Pear Tree Roundabout to Somerton Bridge.

We spent the night in the field, with lots of rabbits and another caravan about 50 yards away. The farmer has kindly opened his gate for us at 6.15 instead of 8.00 am, so I can get under way.

I somehow find my way through all the disruption experienced yesterday, in the Pear Tree Roundabout area, and locate the canal without too much difficulty. Actually, I would have found this very difficult without my Satmap Active 10 device, which clearly shows me the options on screen. Satmap have provided me, free, with a special "Vic's Big Walk" card, which covers my total route between Portsmouth and Blackpool.

Long Lost Fred telephoned yesterday afternoon to arrange a guest appearance on VBW. He had spoken to mine host at the Rock of Gibraltar, a pub on the Oxford Canal and had decided this would be the best place to meet me. That is until he realised how early I would be at that point. In the event, he drives to Lower Heyford, then cycles down the towpath to meet me. When we get back to Lower Heyford, we go to the café there. We take our scones and coffees into the garden, until Fred realises that his yellow cycling shirt is covered in hundreds of small black flying critters. Fred promptly disappears. I can't find him. Eventually, I leave a message with the café staff and re-cross the bridge to the towpath, and there he is. We proceed without incident, except for Fred falling off his bike, to Somerton Bridge, where Gay is waiting for us. A few hundred metres before that point, some people with a Great Dane on a narrowboat whoop and cheer and say well done to me (at this point I have lost Fred again because he has stopped to adjust his brakes). It turns out that these people have been talking to Gay and have left a small donation with her.

After a cup of tea and some coconut macaroons, Fred cycles back to Lower Heyford. I find out later that he fell off his bike again, this time into the canal. I am able to tell Gay that, to match the donation (for Pancreatic Cancer UK) she has received from the boat people, I have a blue note from Peter and Iris. How did that come about? When I reached the Rock of Gibraltar, like all the pubs on the canal at that time of day, it was closed. I asked a couple, who turned out to be Peter and Iris, if there was anywhere open for tea or coffee. They dragged me back to their narrowboat and regaled me with tea and biscuits. We had a nice chat, and as I was leaving they gave me the donation and wished me luck.

I walked 26 kms. VBW total so far 1439.5 kms. Looks as if a small celebration may be called for in a couple of days, when I reach 1500 kms. In fact it looks like Thursday, which could be ideal because Septimus and Mrs Septimus are going to pop up again, stay overnight at the hotel in Brinklow outside which we will be parked, then Sep will walk the Friday stage with me.

Day 53. Somerton Bridge to Claydon Locks.

A very pleasant walk. Gay meets me in Banbury, having sussed out a Costa coffee shop in the shopping mall right next to the canal. I have forsaken Starbucks for Costa when in England. I prefer their coffee, prefer their muffins, prefer their cups as opposed to transport café style mugs, prefer the fact that their premises don't frequently look run-down and seedy. Look to your laurels, Starbucks. I think Costa is only in Britain, but if they go international they could wipe the floor with Starbucks. (I later discover that Costa is already in 40 countries and have a big expansion programme planned).

In the same mall we also find a Jessops camera shop where I am able to replace my camera case. On the previous one, the thing which the strap clips on to had become detached. I had stuck it together with the Uhu which "has been shown on TV" to hold a truck suspended from a crane. Well, it didn't manage to suspend my camera and I have an urgent need of a new case because there is a constant danger of dropping the whole caboodle into the canal. There are expensive cases of all sizes in the shop but the one I buy, made of recycled material, costs me the princely sum of £8.

Today, as usual, I have several conversations with people along the way. My technique is to say, "I have walked here from the Pyrenees!" People invariably want to talk about it. I am happy to do so, and to tell them that I am raising funds for Pancreatic Cancer UK. I don't give a hard sell, but if just a few of them, or only one of them, feels inclined to go away and donate online, it is worth the added time on my journey. Of course another objective is to increase awareness of this appalling illness. And it's nice to talk to people, anyway.

At one lock I speak to Commander John I. Muxworthy, RN. He and his wife are manoeuvring their craft. He is the CEO of the United Kingdom National Defence Association, which has the objective of lobbying for increased, or even adequate funding, for the armed forces. There has been a scandalous rundown in the capabilities, pay and equipment of all three services at the same time as increasing demands on them. And in parallel with dishing out colossal amounts of money to, for instance, bad bankers.

I walked 28 kms today. 1467.5 kms since starting VBW on May 15. 53 days of walking, without a rest.

We are at the Fir Tree Falconry at Warmington, a lovely campsite in a bowl, surrounding a lake. As the name implies, it is also a falconry centre, with birds on display (if you pay) and exhibitions of them flying. Peregrine Falcon, Gyr Falcon, Kestrel, Harris Hawks, European Eagle Owl, Great Horned Owls are just a few of the birds on view.

Day 54. Claydon Locks to Braunston.

For a change – since I arrived in England, that is – the day starts cloudy and windy. It soon becomes humid, although the wind keeps up. The towpath of the canal is surprisingly uneven, banked, and overgrown. Clearly, it is mowed sometimes, but the path between taller vegetation, including nettles and brambles, is pretty narrow. The vegetation is winning the battle at the moment and is encroaching on the path. With the wind whipping said nettles and brambles about this morning, I end the day a bit lacerated as well as lathered.

Soon after setting off I see a fox on the opposite bank, only a few feet away from me. It is carrying some choice morsel in its mouth, presumably taking it home for the young 'uns. I slap leather, camera-wise, but the movement obviously irritates the fox, who high-tails it across the fields. So I don't get a photograph of the fox. But I do get one of a narrowboat called "Alchemy", which makes a nice set with the one a couple of days ago named "Dire Straits".

Sustenance is a bit sparse on the canals, at least in the mornings, when I walk. There are pubs every now and again, but they tend to be closed until lunchtime. I reach one pub at 8.25, which has a sign outside saying, unusually, that it opens at 8.00 am. But there is no sign of life. Several people tell me that there is a café at the bottom of the 9 lock flight approaching Napton, but there is no café to be seen. There is a shop. When I inquire about the ghostly café, it turns out the man who owns the shop used to go to school in Blackpool, where I am headed. He lived in Nelson, East Lancashire, but was a boarder at Arnold School. Not only that, he used to dance with my former aunt by marriage, Jean Mortensen, the wife of Stanley, the man who scored most of the goals in the so-called "Matthews Cup Final".

At Napton itself, the Bridge pub is open – I arrive there at 11.50 so have to wait a few minutes. The very nice lady mine host is from Darlington, where Gay hails from. This young woman boosts my ego no end by several times returning to my table to check whether she heard me right, I can't possibly be 70 years old. This ego-inflation is destined to be punctured the very next morning. Her husband, although South African, has a mother, or maybe grandmother, who comes from Hurworth, just outside Darlington, where Gay was born. Small world!

It is a long walk from Claydon Locks to Braunston. When we were planning this yesterday evening, we realised that I would pass through the 1,500 kms mark today, rather than Thursday as I predicted a few days ago. And so it comes to pass. I walked 35.5 kms and the total progress now is 1503 kms. So we shall have a rare bottle of wine with dinner this evening.

Day 55. Braunston to Brinklow.

They are a miserable lot round here.

By the end of today I have walked 25.5 kms, again on the Oxford Canal. 1528.5 kms since leaving those mist-covered mountains which are home now to me.

Soon after I set out, I see a narrowboat pulling out from the bank. This is really noticeable at that time, because most of the boat people don't seem to crank themselves up until 10 am or so, and I start walking between 6 and 7. I recognise this boat. For a couple of hours yesterday I kept (I accidentally wrote "kep" there but had to change it in case you thought Dolly Parton is writing this book) passing it. When I stopped to proselytise some strangers, it passed me. When I started walking, I passed the boat again. The "driver" did not look up. After several of these incidents, I said something banal like, "We'll have to stop meeting like this". He said, "You've done a few miles". End of conversation. Today I stop and remind him that we had been passing and repassing for much of yesterday. I expect a bit of banter about this. What I get is, "Yes".

As usual, early in the morning, I pass several parked boats which I saw the day before. I see nobody about, but as I pass one of them, I hear a man say, "There's that old boy! The walker." Old boy! I'll have you know a young woman only yesterday would not accept that I am 70! After the fantasy fiction, the reality show.

I come off the canal at Rugby to walk into the town centre for a coffee. This is a bit of a blunder. I hadn't realised just how big Rugby is. It takes me a good hour to reach the city centre. I get a sinking feeling that I will be adding many kms to today's walk. But, after a pleasant pause at Costa, with the help of my Satmap, I manage to strike more or less north west to meet the canal where it swoops round Rugby. I rejoin the canal at Newbold on Avon, where the first thing I have to do is walk through a spectacularly decorated tunnel which is a credit to whoever conceived and executed it.

The day had started out with spits and spots of rain, as John Kettley used to say on the weather forecast, but turned out bright and hot. We are now parked up at the Bull's Head in Brinkley. We have been reunited with Mr and Mrs Septimus, who have just arrived to stay at the pub tonight. Septimus is walking on with me to Atherstone tomorrow.

Oh, the miserable bit! The man on the boat may not have been a local, but most of the people in Rugby seemed to walk past with their eyes firmly fixed to the floor in case they should accidentally speak to, or even look at, a stranger. Like English people abroad.

Oh, OK, not most of them – some of them. I spoke to a number of very friendly people. The jury will disregard my remarks. But a couple of fishermen did not even turn round or answer when I passed and spoke to them.

Day 56. Brinklow to Atherstone.

Not much to say about today's walk. Too long, at 35 kms. Especially in the very hot conditions. Not enough sustenance available on the way.

When we set off, we are still on the Oxford Canal. At Hawkesbury Junction, the Oxford Canal finishes where it joins with the Coventry Canal at a t-junction. It should be quite simple, the Coventry canal at this point runs south to Coventry or north to Atherstone. But the junction is a bit visually confusing, or at least it was to us. We were at least one kilometre on our way to Coventry before we realised that we had gone wrong. As we walked back, this gave us a second chance to have a look at some striking metal swan sculptures on a bridge just south of the junction. We could also see where we had gone wrong. The last bit of the Oxford Canal heads south, so that it is virtually parallel with the northern arm of the Coventry Canal, which at that point was behind our right shoulders and invisible. This little adventure adds 2 kms to a long day.

We come off the canal at one spot – Chivers Coton – where we had learned there was a craft centre with 20-odd craft shops and a café. We home in on the café, of course, where, in addition to our tea and buns, I receive a donation from the lady behind the counter. Interesting that the church in this village was built by German prisoners-of-war. Shame that we have to add to our distance by diverting from the canal for this welcome sit-down.

Septimus seems to specialise in joining me for overlong walks on very hot days. I assume this is not deliberate because he doesn't seem to enjoy those conditions any more than I do.

I receive a 'phone call on the way, from Nicola in Iddly, who told me that Fabrizio is in Malmo, Sweden. A few minutes later we walk past a boat called "Malmo".

Today is the end of the 8th week of walking without a day off. At the end of today's long walk I am a bit bloody fed up. It has been one of those days where I was tired for the whole distance. Halfway through I received a text message from Gay asking if we could give an estimate of when we would be at the finish. She normally makes a point of saying not to worry about her waiting, it will take however long it takes. I fume that I am not doing this to a bloody timetable. I want to stop and talk to people and ideally get them to donate. I want to stop and have rests when I can, and some days I need them more than others. I am bloody annoyed about it. I overreact and snap at Gay when she and Pat meet us at the end. This is most unfair, Gay is being a marvellous support to me. It doesn't help that a dog bites my hand just as we see them. Am I cracking under the pressure, with two weeks to go? This is the first day I have felt or behaved like this.

We arrive in Atherstone. Day's distance 35 kms. Total so far 1563.5 kms. Gay has already parked up at the campsite so Pat runs us over there. Paul and Pat go home immediately. I am not sure whether this is because they are alarmed by my snappiness., or whether Paul is eager to get home and sink his teeth into the enormous pork pie which Pat has presented to him.

In the evening we see my old friend Bill Davies. We are quite near to where he lives. Bill comes round to the caravan site to pick us up and take us out for dinner. Sadly, Bill recently lost his wife Val to cancer. This is the first time I have seen him since then. He seems very resilient. He drives us in his Jaguar to a pub about two and half miles from our very rural campsite. The pub was built in 1245, and the heights of the ceilings and doors reflected that. Some of the old wattle and daub is visible where the wall is replaced by a glass panel for that purpose. We have a good time with Bill, who insists on paying, then goes home and makes a generous donation to the cause.

Chapter 15. The Ninth Week.

Day 57. Atherstone to Whittington.

Just coming up to a place called Polesworth, which I have never heard of before. I have already walked 6 kms today. It is very hot, like yesterday.

The canal goes south at Tamworth, then west and north again. I come off before it dips too far south and walk into the centre of Tamworth to the Ventura Retail Park where I go to a very light and spacious Costa. The girl who serves me is really beautiful, both visually and in personality. She also has good customer interface skills. I get into conversation with her and some people in the queue about what I am doing and the girl (a different one) who is making my coffee says that one of her relatives died of pancreatic cancer, the man in front of me said his brother died of it. So I dish out the cards.

I walk from there, west and north, using my Satmap Active 10 to navigate myself back to the canal up a very quiet road past a farm, where I can rejoin the canal and head more or less due north.

As I am passing Hopwas village, somewhere near Lichfield, two chaps on boats are talking together but stop that to greet me. One of them says – twice – he will light a candle for me. That's not the first time I have heard this during VBW – I can't remember where the other one was. I'd sooner he made a donation than lit a candle.

I get going again and a couple of dogs come hurtling off a boat. A small dog first, then a bigger one. Both coming straight at me in attack mode. So my right shoe delivers a swift uppercut under the chin of the big one and he lands on his back and takes an eight count. Maybe I should take up Thai boxing. They retreat very fast, the bastards. Earlier today a Newfoundland had a go at me. Christ! That could have done some damage. Fortunately the fellow had managed to shorten the lead. So many dog owners walk along with their mutts on a long lead when other people are about. They have no control over them.

I am just emerging from under a bridge, on the towpath, when a fellow comes running down from the bridge, facing away from me, and runs off. I swear he was wearing just a loin cloth. Maybe it was Lord Greystoke, aka Tarzan, out on a training run. I ask a young couple at a boat what on earth he was wearing. "Just his knickers, I think", says the girl.

Gay picks me up at a pub on the canal where some sort of dragon boat race is just about to start, with all sorts of young people wearing odd costumes.

Today I entered Staffordshire, and nostalgia territory. I have lived in Staffs and Cheshire and Lancashire, the next two counties, for much of my life, so will be meeting people and seeing places which will inevitably stir up memories.

I didn't expect that to start with the view I had for some time today, of the enormous television transmitter aerial near Lichfield. Jim Gregson and I sat in a layby on the A5 for 2 hours in the very early 70s, or possibly late 60s, staring at that mast and waiting for a rescue vehicle to tow my inoperative car to a garage in Stafford (that drive was quite exciting, I remember, on the back end of a rope).

I seem to have swiftly progressed from crossing 1500 kms on Wednesday, to nudging 1600 kms on Saturday. Today's walk, again in very hot circumstances, was 28 kms. The total is now 1591.5 kms. I hope to be having some shorter walks in the remaining 13 days, maybe even a couple of days off so that Gay and I can do some nostalgia sightseeing in V-Force One.

In the evening we are taken out to dinner at an excellent Chinese restaurant in Lichfield. John Hayfield has already driven himself and his lady Sandra up from Devon to their home on the edge of the Cotswolds. Then he drives to Lichfield and on to our campsite 26 kms north, picks us up, drives us in to Lichfield, brings us back to the campsite, then he and Sandra go back to the Cotswolds. Unbelievable! You will be pleased to know that in the middle of all that, we had a splendid time at the restaurant.

Day 58. Whittington to Wolseley Bridge.

Last night's campsite was actually the place where I am going to finish today's walk. That's how far away it is from where I finished yesterday, but we just couldn't find anywhere nearer. And yet this morning, on the way back to today's start, and yesterday's finish, to the east of Lichfield, we saw a campsite in Lichfield. It is not listed anywhere we have looked. We didn't find it on the internet, although we searched.

The campsite we are at is a bit primitive. It is basically a fishing centre with a field and electricity points. There is a toilet block which is further away from us than the entrance. No showers, nothing else. Not to mention an awful telephone signal for the internet.

This morning Gay drives me back to yesterday's finishing point near Whittington and deposits me next to the towing path of the Coventry Canal. I hop on the path and head north. She heads in the direction of Rugely for a desperately needed launderette. The combination of this hot weather and my own antics is producing lots of damp kit. As we are not registered ammonia producers a pile of it is urgently in need of a washing machine. I learn later that fortunately Gay found one and all is, as they used to say on the toothpaste adverts, clean and sparkling.

One of my first impressions of England on any visit is, like most people, the amount of traffic. This time, walking, I have particularly noticed not just the number of cars but the speed. Everybody goes so fast. Such a high proportion of big, powerful cars. Everybody is in a hurry, got to get there. Fortunately, on the canals, I am now away from that but the high car density still has a visual impact. Some modern housing estates are close to the canal. One thing that really hits me about this is that, apart from the fact that the houses are crammed so close together, the whole area is littered with cars. The planners seem to have taken no account of the fact that people have cars. The norm for a house is two cars, frequently three or four. There is usually a garage but because houses don't have much storage area, the garage is used for anything but cars, so all the cars are outside. The only place planned for cars is the garage itself and maybe the bit of drive approaching it – one car length maybe. The result is that the whole road, nose to tail, on a brand new housing estate, is covered with cars. And no pavements. Another thing about traffic is the constant noise, the constant roar, of vehicular noise. You can hear this in the most rural areas. I have been in very few places in England where I haven't been aware of that noise, all the time, in the background. And of course when you are near a motorway or a fast and busy main road – I don't mean next to it, when you are near it, the noise is deafening, and yet people live there – it's appalling.

There are two cafes at Fradley Junction, neither of them open until ten. It is half past eight when I get there. I ask several people on the towpath if there is a decent café in Rugeley but the only answer I get is Morrisons supermarket, just off the canal, the only café they know about that will be open on a Sunday. So I go there to find press-a-button coffee. This is served by the counter staff but it could just as easily come from a slot machine. I have a pecan Danish, which is quite tasty. The young girl who takes my money says that a member of her family died of pancreatic cancer and that she will donate. She is only a slip of a thing. I wouldn't have thought she had any money to donate. She asks me to leave some cards by the till, so I do so.

I pass one moored vehicle which is flying two New Zealand flags – the official one with the union jack in the corner, and the one which could possibly replace it, with the silver fern. Some time later, I catch up with a moving boat, which has a New Zealand name. It turns out that the previous owners had been New Zealanders. Of the current crew, the young lady I am speaking to, when she learns of my mission, tells me that she was born in Blackpool. In Kendal Avenue. This is small worldsville again – several of my late first wife's relatives lived in that street, including her mother and father.

It is strange walking back to the campsite I left at 6.30 this morning, but here I am. It is not too far from the canal path. Tomorrow I will walk on to Stone, where I lived for a while in the early 60s.

Today's walk was 26.5 kms, I am now walking up the Trent and Mersey Canal, and kilometres to date are 1,618, which, for the Luddites, is well over 1,000 miles.

Today there is an extraordinary donation to Pancreatic Cancer UK on my

JustGiving page. The sum is £540, which was given by an 18 year old boy in Dublin. The message from him which failed to appear on the JustGiving page is as follows:
Dear Vic,
Last week, for my 18th Birthday my parents bought me a parachute jump. I thought I would take the opportunity to raise money for your cancer research charity in support of your efforts and in memory of my Grandmother. As the jump was paid for by my parents, every donation I got could go directly to charity. I collected a total that was the equivalent of £540 in sterling, so here it is.
Everyone was very supportive over here, and they feel that your walk is a very noble and selfless cause! I hope the money I raised will prove to be a nice contribution to your journey!
I hope to see you soon; we will try to meet you along your way next Saturday.
Your friend,
Rowan Moorkens O'Reilly
Rowan is an extraordinary boy, if you need telling that after this amazing piece of fundraising. Among other things, he has been on an astronaut training course in America.

Day 59. Wolseley Bridge to Stone.

We were sitting in V-Force One yesterday evening, minding our own business, when I saw a hot-air balloon looming over us. We went outside to get a better look, and noticed that two other balloons had already gone past without us noticing. They are such a beautiful sight.

Despite all that excitement, we slept well. For the first time in years, Gay has been sleeping well every night during VBW. It's a strange thing that, ever since we moved to live in "Cathar Country" she has rarely had a good night's sleep. Even more odd that this seems to apply to most of the women we know who live in the same area. I never have any trouble, even when not walking 30 kms a day.

We awake this morning to the good news that the heat wave is over. The weather man says there will be rain today, but nothing sustained – I realise later that I must have accidentally been listening to a comedy show. It is spitting when I set off, but after half an hour or so it starts lashing down. This goes on for some hours. The towpath is mainly grass, so my shoes and socks soon become uncomfortably sodden. The rest of me is as snug as a bug in a poncho.

As I approach Stone, I see the Soup Dragon striding towards me. This is not a surprise. Tonight we shall be staying in his house in Newcastle-under-Lyme. The original plan was for Soupie to walk today's stage with me, but he sustained an injury which put paid to that. So he parked up in Stone and walked along the canal towpath to meet me.

We find Gay and have a coffee in Stone, then he clears off to take care of business while we do a bit of nostalgising in Stone. I lived here for 4 years or so in the very early 60s. After Derek (the Soup Dragon's alias) has gone, we drive over to Walton, a suburb of Stone where I take a photograph of the tiny flat where I once lived. My eldest daughter Karen, although she lived there as a baby, will not remember the place.

Then we drive to Derek's home where we have the rest of the day off. Amazingly, after 59 days walking, we have tomorrow off as well.

I walked 22 kms and the total VBW distance covered so far is 1640. I have stopped recounting ascents since I hit the canal towpaths which, as I understand physics, should be flat.

Day 60. Rest Day!

I am dawdling about now because I have plenty of time in hand. I could probably get to Blackpool this weekend if I just continued straight on up the canals, but that would ruin the concept of walking back through 70 years of life in 70 days. It would also ruin the plans of people who have come from overseas to witness my arrival at the house where I was born.

I have cut out the side trips to nostalgia land, or at least the walking version of those, which I only ever intended to do if I had lots of time to spare. As it happens, although I am ahead of the game, if I now walked off to Leek, et cetera, I would be really pushed for time, but as we are now going to have a day off to drive to those places, I shall still have time in hand when I reach Lancashire.

There will be no walking today, for the first time since May 15th. It is now July 13th, with 10 days to go.

"The Pithead bath's a supermarket now ..."

So sings Max Boyce. I suppose that is progress. Things move on.

Well, the first flat I had, the one I shared with the late Jeff Bardsley, over the newsagents in Huntbach Street, Hanley, is a carpark now. Big disappointment of the day. They paved paradise and put up a parking lot, you know.

In Hanley centre today we were surrounded by eateries and yet I remember that when I went to live in that flat in Huntbach Street with Jeff Bardsley, so far as we knew there was only one place in the whole of Stoke on Trent, which claimed to be a city, where we could get a meal in the evening. It happened to be at the bottom of the street.

I get good pictures of the first school Karen went to in Werrington, and the first house I owned, also in Werrington, which is where Nicola was born. Later the girls are delighted with the pictures.

Then we drive over to Leek. We have a bit of a poke around the town centre and take lunch in a café there. Again it was very interesting to see all the eateries in what used to be a one-sandwich town.

We had been intending to meet a gentleman who now runs the Lib Dems in this area. I have been in touch with him a couple of times. I, with a couple of chums, founded the Liberal Party in that constituency and it would have been interesting to meet and compare notes, especially now the Lib Dems are in government for the first time since WW2. Unfortunately we were going to be there late morning and he had to leave to visit a friend in hospital in Nottingham and he was delayed coming back so we weren't able to meet in the afternoon. He rang us in the evening on our campsite in the Roaches, where we had an awful signal and were cut off several times.

I lived in other places in this area, but sadly I do not have time to visit them all. When I first arrived in Staffordshire I was in "digs" with Mrs Phillips at 337 Uttoxeter Road at Blythe Bridge. Mrs Phillips is responsible for the fact that I don't like malt bread very much * although that wasn't always so. She gave us some one day, when we came in from the evening shift. I happened to mention that I liked it and after that we seemed to have it morning, noon and night until I was sick of it. She was only doing her best to be kind and to make us feel at home. Another food problem there was that she would make a pot of tea and then put it in the oven to keep warm. This was one of the old black ovens built around the fireplace. The problem was that when she offered you a cup of tea you didn't know whether she was about to make a fresh pot or would haul one out of the oven, where it could have been lurking for a couple of hours. Two hour old tea is not to be recommended.

I shared a room at Uttoxeter Road with Peter Symes. He was in his mid-twenties. I was nineteen at the time. Peter used to have nightmares. In the middle of one of these he leapt out of his bed, where presumably he had been lying down fast asleep, across the foot of my bed, at the same time as emitting an awful yell. He couldn't possibly have repeated the feat while awake.

Some time later I found myself staying on a farm in Cheadle, not far from where I worked. The farm belonged to the family Beard.

The Beards were a race of giants. The two sons living on the farm were several inches over six feet tall. One, who had fair hair, was Li'l Abner to the life. He was the very pleasant fellow who once asked me if I would come and hold a calf for him, while he treated its hoof for an infection. When we reached the byre, I couldn't see a calf, only an almost fully-grown bull. No matter how much I looked around, this turned out to be the calf. Li'l Abner asked me to lay it down and hold it there while he attended to it. Seeing my blank look, he grabbed it by the horns and pushed its head and shoulders to the ground. I then had to hold it, with my knee in its shoulder, one hand on a horn and the other hand in its mouth. I felt as if the creature could have thrown me off without too much trouble. It rolled its eyes a lot and looked as if that was its intention, but it took its medicine like a bull. When Li'l invited me to release it, it jumped to its feet, looked at us, considered revenge, but shambled off to join its colleagues.

Day 61. Stone to Stoke on Trent.

We leave the campsite behind and head back to Stone. The Roaches, dramatic rock formations, cover quite an area. Once upon a time some of the fell runners from our athletics club were on a training run hereabouts and were stunned to see some wallabies hopping along. Their astonishment was not just because the marsupials were much faster than the runners, and clearly capable of winning any fell race they entered. The lads had never heard that the critters existed here. But they have been around for many a long year. I remember that in the terrible winter of 1962/3 the macropods were expected to die out, but they survived and thrived.

We have breakfast at Costa in Stone. Being here over the last couple of days has enabled me to see how much the town has changed. The High Street is now pedestrianised –and it looks so much better. But the main employers of my day have disappeared – the glass factory of Quickfit and Quartz, the Lotus shoe factory, at least one of the two breweries. It's a busy place, though, with lots of traffic coming through, but then so is everywhere in Britain .

I pick up the baton I dropped here on Monday, then press on up the Trent and Mersey Canal.

It is strange to be walking along the canal path in Stone. I lived here for several years and I can't remember ever having walked on the canal bank at that time.

There are lots of canal boats again. Some of them are actually moving, although I am starting later this morning because we had to drive over from Leek, plus only having a short walking day ahead of me

Somebody a couple of days ago told me that Terry Darlington's famous narrowboat, in which he crossed to France and which starred in the book "Narrow dog to Carcassonne", had been burned out by some vandals in Stone.

After a few kms I come to Barlaston, where I pause to take a photograph of the Plume of Feathers pub. This is probably the only pub in the world which I, not being a drinker, can be said to have frequented for a while. At a particularly turbulent period of my life, in about 1970, I was in this pub a few times. One of the regulars was a young man, clearly highly strung and excitable, who was known to other regulars, for obvious reasons, as "Loony Bassett". He was always involved in arguments with anybody, and of course they would deliberately wind him up. Unfortunately, his looniness had very bad consequences for three young French people.

I had heard Loony say that he used an air rifle to shoot birds from his bedroom window. I also heard him announce that, if he were to kill somebody, he would use a gun, to make sure of the job. Not long after this, I was in the car one night when a news bulletin announced that a young French trio had been killed where they were camping in Delamere Forest, near Chester. A description of the suspect followed – it was clearly Loony Bassett.

The full story emerged the next day. Loony had taken a day trip to Rhyl or one of the resort towns on the North Wales coast. At a fun-fair, he had heard the French youngsters laughing. Being of a paranoid persuasion, he thought they were laughing at him, although they had probably not given him a glance or a thought. He stole a rifle from a shooting gallery, then followed them all the way back to their campsite, many miles away. I put it to the jury, your honour, that this shows evidence of premeditation. After slaughtering them, he went home, or thereabouts, drove to Barlaston Downs, a secluded local beauty spot, and gassed himself, using a tube attached to his exhaust pipe. Presumably the tube was not just lying around, so it seems he had given some forethought to that, as well.

When I am taking a photograph of Loony's pub, I explain to an old man at a house a couple of doors away, why I am doing so. I tell him the story of Loony Bassett. Amazingly, although this man, older than me, has lived in the area for all or most of his life, he does not know the story. So poor old Loony does not even get lasting fame out of his murderous exploits.

But I am not the only one who remembers it. Later in the day, I mention this story on my blog. My memory has told me that there were two dead French youngsters, a couple. Dale Heighway also remembered the incident but thought there were three French people, He searched the internet and came up with a BBC report of the incident. This revealed that Dale was correct about the number of slain. Michael Basset, 24, was found in a maroon Ford Escort . There was a pipe from the exhaust into the car and Bassett was cradling a gun with a confession written on a local newspaper beside him. He admitted shooting dead Monique Liebert, 22, her sister Claudine Liebert, 20 – both teachers from Fontenay-le-Comte in northern France – and Claudine's fiance Daniel Berland, 20, a student from St Medard des Pres near Fontenay. His letter claimed: "They provoked me so I taught them a lesson." Fontenay le Comte is a town which we frequently use as an overnight staging post when driving, instead of walking, to the ferry ports in Normandy.

As Dale points out, the BBC report carries the date 14th July 1971. Today, as I stand outside the Plume of Feathers, taking photographs and remembering the case, it is 14th July 2010. Is that spooky, or what? Dale also mentions that 14th July 1971 was the birth date of "a man who has been in the world's eye in the last week". This was Howard Webb who refereed the (soccer) world cup final last Sunday!

I press on. I pass the famous Wedgewood pottery, which is now in Barlaston "set in 250 acres of lush parkland". There is an excellent visitor centre, a huge outlet shop and an award-winning restaurant and tea shop. The Wedgewood factory originated in Etruria, in Stoke on Trent, very close to where I will finish today's walk. Josiah

Wedgewood was largely responsible for the building of this canal.

My walk today is only 16.5 kms, total so far 1656.5 kms. We park at the premises of Towtal, in Heron Cross, Stoke on Trent. Towtal are members of an organisation called Motorhome Stopovers. This consists mainly of pubs which welcome campervans overnight on their carparks, in the hope that people will emerge from the campervans and consume food or beverage on their premises. Towtal mend campervans, they make trailers to carry tiny cars behind campervans, and they sell secondhand campervans. I am not clear what trade they would expect to get as a result of one sleeping on their premises. Maybe just the possibility that you could use one of their other services. And maybe it works. We are here because it is ideally situated on my walk and there seems to be not a campsite nearby. We are certainly pleased with them already. As a result of a sudden gust of wind and our ignorance, the awning on the side of V-Force One has not been in a working condition since early in the trip. Thanks to a quick bit of wizardry by the head of the workshops, it is now fully functional.

Day 62. Stoke on Trent to Congleton.

Morning of Thursday 15th July. I set out to walk from Heron Cross to Kidsgrove and then up to Congleton. Although we last night planned a route which involved me going back onto the canals, I decided at the last minute this morning that I would walk up through the towns of Stoke on Trent because I will see a lot of things which are familiar.

The amended route will take me through Fenton, Hanley, Burslem, Tunstall, Goldenhill, and Kidsgrove, where I will get on to the Macclesfield Canal to Congleton.

Although the forecast was talking rain, and it has rained sporadically during the night, there is actually, despite the clouds, a blue sky and I am already quite warm. I didn't put any sun lotion on and I forgot to bring my hat. Foolish.

I walk through the middle of Hanley for the second time this week. It is a tangle of new roads which I have never seen before. Once again Satmap comes to the rescue. When I first came to live in the Potteries, Stoke on Trent was celebrating its first 50 years as a city. It was struggling to live up to that title. Dining out was almost impossible. Now, the posters are up, proclaiming the 100 years celebration. As Ray Bonneville sings – "Where did it go – the time I mean?" And once again I am amazed that Hanley seems to be knee-deep in eateries. Costa, which is inside a locked shopping complex, is not open until 9 am, so I settle for a cappuccino in Caffe Nero. This is progress!

It is 40 years since I left the area and as with anywhere you return to after such a long time it is so different, especially when new roads carve the place up. Also, I had forgotten how hilly this area is   it is just one hill after another.

I walk down Waterloo Road between Hanley and Burslem. There are big houses where the rich used to aspire to live, as in Arnold Bennett's Clayhanger trilogy, which is largely about those aspirations. In those books this was Trafalgar Road. More or less as I was leaving the area in the 70s the big houses were turning into multi-occupancy places for immigrants and now I notice a lot of them have been knocked down and replaced by three story modern blocks.

I manage to get a haircut at Goldenhill. A nice lad, from Congleton. He tells me he was driven out of Congleton by the parking charges which have been introduced, as is so often the case, ill-advisedly, and which of course took away the custom, people preferring to go somewhere with free parking. They metered paradise and drove the business away. Clearly, he was particularly disturbed by the disappearance from Congleton of the genus Clientus Barberus. He only charges me £5 and says he will donate on the website.

I walk out of the shop and am on my way when he comes running after me with my spectacles. I always take these off when having a haircut because of all the little bits of hair which otherwise cling to the lenses. What I don't understand is how I managed to find my way through the door without them. I hadn't even noticed they were missing! I am sure that crashing into the first lamp post would have alerted me to the problem.

As I approach Kidsgrove, I remember Dale's warning about the "Kidsgrove Boggart". If, as originally planned, I had walked today along the Trent and Mersey Canal, I would have reached the Harecastle Tunnel, where the Boggart is said to lurk.

Originally, there were two tunnels. One, built by Brindley, is 2,880 yards long. The later one, built by Telford, was 2,926 yards. They both still exist, but only the Telford tunnel is navigable. There is no towing path because the tunnel is not wide enough. Indeed, there is a one-way system in force and boats are sent through in groups, alternating northbound and southbound. Because there was no towing path, before the days of powered canal craft, the boatmen had to leg their way through the tunnel, lying on the roof of their boat and pushing on the sides of the tunnel with their feet. It could take up to three hours to get through the tunnel. The boat horses had to be taken over the top of the hill, which is where I would have had to walk today.

There are many versions of the Kidsgrove Boggart story, all associated with the Harecastle Tunnel. This is one:

In Victorian times the canal was in regular use. A woman's husband went up to London to make his fortune. He left his barge behind and told his wife when I send a letter that I have been successful I want you to come to London in the boat.

Many years later she received the long-awaited letter from her husband saying that he had hit the big time and wanted her to come to London as arranged. She immediately had her things packed and prepared the barge. She went into a Kidsgrove pub and asked if anyone would be willing to take her to London on the old narrowboat. She eventually found two men and they agreed on an amount of money for the service.

They boarded the barge and entered the old Harecastle tunnel. As they reached the middle of the tunnel they both attacked and raped her. Suddenly she slipped off the side of the barge and her head was ripped from her body in an instant. The men were eventually caught for the terrible crime and were hanged in Kidsgrove. The husband never saw his wife again and they say her head was never found. People say she moans because she searches for her head so that she can begin her journey back to London to find her husband.

Fortunately, having changed my route, I have avoided the possibility of meeting the subject of this sad tale.

In Kidsgrove I make a slight diversion to visit my ex-brother in law Ray, who I have not seen for well over 20 years. He seems pleased to see me but neglects to mention the kettle. Ray, known to his friends for some reason as Wack, was a very accomplished amateur boxer when he was a young man. I credit him with inspiring the start of my running career, which was provoked by seeing him set off for his nightly training runs.

Ray's home is very near to the factory where I started my third career, with International Computers Limited. Actually, when I joined the company it was called English Electric Leo Marconi Computers Limited. That was such a mouthful that it had to be merged with International Tabulator Limited to become ICL. This was a move encouraged by the UK government to create the flagship of British computer manufacturing. Unfortunately, subsequent changes of ownership and mergers have seen it now become part of Fujitsu, a flagship of Japanese computer manufacturing.

I leave Ray's Butt Lane address and rejoin the Trent and Mersey Canal for a few yards before climbing the steps to the Macclesfield Canal. In Congleton we shall be staying overnight with Big Tone and Mu. Their house faces on to this very canal.

I meet a lovely man, Graham Green. He is fishing, for the first time in 20 years, although he seems to be rather hoping he will not catch anything, not wanting to gain his own pleasure at the expense of giving pain to another creature. He says it is a fantastic thing that I am doing and wishes me well. He then gives me £20 for the fund. Later I put it onto the JustGiving page, with that message from him.

Somewhere along this stretch of canal VBW enters Cheshire, the penultimate county. I reach the home of Big Tone and Mu, having walked 29 kms today and 1685.5 so far. We spend a very convivial afternoon and evening, a'reminiscin' and a'chawin'. Tone and I used to work together in the 70s, at the very ICL I mentioned above.

Day 63. Congleton to Wilmslow.

The road to Wilmslow from Congleton is the very busy A34, much of it without pavements, but with lots of bends – in other words, good Vic-killing territory. It seems a bit early to terminate VBW in that way, so my navigation officer has planned a route to the west of the A34, necessarily a bit longer, but with the priority on safety. Mainly side roads and walking paths. Gay's planning is great, the roads are quiet and safe. But it seems that nobody else has ever spotted the paths on the map. Certainly nobody has ever walked them. There is no worn bit on the ground, the grass is long and, because of the rain which becomes heavy, extremely wet, as are my shoes and socks very quickly. Many of the farm gates are locked, even when accompanied by a signpost clearly saying a footpath goes through them. And in many places, the "path" is completely overgrown by nettles and brambles. No sooner has the nettle rash on my legs subsided, than I am into another lot of nettles and another rash.

When I near Alderley Edge, I discover that a bypass of the town is under construction. This is good, it is badly needed. But it is not good for my walk. Forward progress is an impossible dream. It means I have to retrace my steps and find another way around. This adds a few kilometres. When I finally reach Alderley Edge and Costa, for a much needed coffee, I am not sure I will be allowed in, I am so sodden. I find myself sitting next to a couple who live four doors away from my former home in Dean Drive, the address to which I am headed in order to take a photograph.

I trudge past the offices where I was based when I was a Northern Regional Manager in Dataskil, a computer services subsidiary of ICL. The offices were over some shops. At one time one of these was a Wurlitzer outlet. One of our young secretaries, Jenny Muir, was looking out of the window when a Rolls Royce pulled up. She asked who was getting out of it. I went over and identified him as Dick Emery, a very popular TV comedian at the time. Jenny had never heard of him but this did not stop her going downstairs and intercepting him with the immortal line, "Hello Dick, how's your mother?" Dick Emery was so captivated by Jenny's cheek that he whisked her away in his Rolls Royce and took her for lunch.

A little later I reach the Bluebell BMW salesroom at Dean Row. I call in to see if an old friend still works there. As I enter the portals, my phone rings for a newspaper interview, so I pop outside again and am interviewed by the Wigan Observer against the roar of traffic pulling up to and leaving the traffic lights. Eventually I find that the friend is still with the company, in a senior capacity, but not in that building.

I press on into Dean Drive to take a photo of my old house. So many memories as I enter the street. In the mid or late 70s the country suffered a very cold winter. I remember the Soup Dragon telling me that when he was staying with friends in Shropshire, his shampoo froze in the bathroom. One of my memories of that winter is of me returning from a long run in the snow. I met the milkman as I ran into Dean

Drive. He started laughing, which is when I found that I had earrings. I sweat a lot while running, even when the temperature is below freezing. The sweat had run from my ears and frozen there, eventually forming an icicle on each ear.

There is a car parked on the drive of my ex-residence, so I think I had better warn the owner that I will be taking a picture, and that it will not be for nefarious purposes. He is really friendly and interested in what I am doing. He invites me in, happy to show me round the house. But by then I am well behind schedule, aware that Gay has been waiting for ages and that she has eaten no lunch.

I meet her at the garden centre opposite where Dean Drive meets the main road again, then we hot-wheel it to Altrincham and the home of our old friends Jean and Bernard Dolan, where we are to spend the night.

We all used to be members of Altrincham and District Athletics Club. The club's training track is within strolling distance of Maison Dolan. Bernard was not a great one for training, but he was famous for more than fifteen minutes as the man who used to stop for a cigarette partway through marathon races.

During the afternoon, while writing up my blog, I find there is no photo of the Dean Drive house in my camera! So I may have to do Vic's Big Walk all over again. But no, Nick Mellor, the current owner of my old house, not only sends me a photograph but invites me to visit any time.

I have walked 31.5 mainly very wet kms, bringing the total so far to 1717 kms.

This is the end of the 9th week of Vic's Big Walk. Not far now!

Chapter 16. The tenth and last week.

Day 64. Wilmslow to Warburton Toll Bridge.

Saturday, the beginning of the final week of VBW. Gay asked me last night, "Is your bladder OK". I thought, bloody hell, have I been wetting the bed, or something?" She meant is the water bladder in my rucksack full of water and ready for action. I said there was plenty of water in it. This morning when I picked up the rucksack to go, she pointed out that the bottom of the bag was wet. We examined it and found out that the bladder was leaking so I have had to ditch it, which is a bit of a shame. It is so strange that this should happen just after she asked if my bladder is OK. But so kind of the bladder to wait until we were out of the hot weather, when it was so desperately needed.

Gay drives me back to Wilmslow, where I finished yesterday's walk. Within minutes the sunny start turns to heavy rain. My route takes me under the runways at Manchester Airport to Hale, where Gay and I once lived. I make a small diversion to gaze at the house, which surprisingly displays no blue plaque, and to take a photograph. I continue down Hermitage Road and rejoin Hale Road, the main road from Wilmslow to Altincham. At this junction there is a cemetery. Gay and I found a tombstone in there once, which bears the name "Emperor Boss" and a date. Ever since, we have wondered who was Emperor Boss, and how did he get this name? Was he indeed an Emperor? Or even a boss? Since completing the walk, and while preparing this book, I have at last discovered the truth, thanks to a report on the Internet from Friends of Stamford Park.

It seems that there were 1900 Gypsies in the area. Emperor Boss was one of their leaders. He abandoned horse-dealing and settled down as a furniture remover and firewood dealer. At the end of his days he was buried in the grave which has puzzled us for so long.

I walk into the centre of Hale. Our friend Marcello's restaurant was here, but Marcello sadly died in recent years. We have visited his grave outside his home town of Bagna di Lucca in Italy. It is in a wonderfully scenic position in a tiny graveyard atop a Tuscan hill, with magnificent views for miles around.

After taking sustenance at Costa, and doing some proselytising there for the cause, (and receiving two promises of donations, only one of which came to pass) I walk through Dunham Massey Park on the way to Warburton. Our training runs frequently took us through here when we were local residents. Dunham Park is a National Trust Property – an old "stately home" in extensive grounds, with deer popping up behind every tree. It was formerly the home of the last Earl of Stamford.

The village of Dunham Massey contains 45 listed buildings.

In the park the sun appears briefly. I bump into Sir James Anderton, the ex-Chief Constable of Manchester. He was a very controversial holder of that post – a professed Christian who claimed to speak regularly with God. He was very outspoken on the subjects of homosexuality and AIDS, famously quoted as saying that those with AIDS were "swirling in a cesspit of their own making."

But he is all affability. He exclaims, "You have brought the sunshine". I tell him I have brought it from the Pyrenees, a slight variation from my usual opening line – I am nothing if not adaptable. We have a chat about what I am doing. He and his friend are fascinated by the VBW project and as I walk away he calls after me, "You must write that book!" Well, here it is, Sir James.

The chat takes place in a brief interval in what is a pretty wet walk. Most of this week has been wet, in fact. Before that, there were weeks of very hot weather and a hose-pipe ban was instituted in the North-West of England only a few days ago. I think it was the same day that the rain started. We are expecting a bonus for having changed things so dramatically. There has previously been some debate on my blog about a suitable theme song for VBW. I have been leaning towards "Walking in the rain." Sir James, after I explain that I am walking backwards through my life from where I am now to where I started, reminds me that Spike Milligan sang "I'm walking backwards to Christmas". I point out that I have no intention of walking across the Irish Sea, as in the next line of that song.

I arrive at our camp next to the Warburton Toll Bridge over the Manchester Ship Canal. I know I have been on a bit of a nostalgia tour diversion for the past few days, but at this point I have a nostalgia attack which takes me completely by surprise. It is only as I approach the bridge that I make the connection.

My first job was as a Radio Officer in the Merchant Navy. My first trip started in Manchester and, on the way to Canada, the M/V Manchester Spinner passed down this very Ship Canal, and under this very bridge, on its way to the sea. Of course the canal was built to link Manchester, then the world capital of cotton processing – King Cotton, as it was known – to the sea near Liverpool. It is little used now, and despite its fame its useful working life was much less than one century – it is rather like myself in that respect.

Distance covered was 24 kms. VBW total to date 1741 kms.

In the afternoon we have a visit from our friends Evelyn, Ian and Rowan. They live in Ireland, are on their way to Cockermouth for a job (Evelyn and Ian are both environmental scientists), and have made a diversion to see us. I mentioned Rowan earlier, when he made an extraordinary donation of over £500 to my fund. This is the second biggest donation and Rowan is still a schoolboy – the bigger donation was from a millionaire. We walk down to a local pub and have an early dinner before they head north. The pub owners have left their 18-year old son in charge. Our visitors tell him what I am doing, and how far I have walked. He just keeps saying, "Bloody Hell!" He must say it seven or eight times.

Day 65. Warburton Toll Bridge to Dover Lock.

Today is the first of my 3 days with the Walters Walking Club. The first Walter I came across was Dale Heighway, who walked with me in Normandy. He and Ken Critchley came to me through my blog and my JustGiving donations page. In the planning stages, I had not decided how best to route myself from Cheshire into Lancashire – if I stuck to the canals I would waste many kilometres. Dale told me that Frank Dawber, leader of the Walters, would work out a route for me and also arrange a relay of Walters to guide me, passing me from one to the other like a Pony Express parcel. All the Walters are ex-Pilkington Glass employees who Worked All Life and Took Early Retirement.

The first of the Walters in England, Gerry Miller, rolls up for the first half of today's walk and amazes us by saying that he grew up in the next street but one to Septimus (who has also arrived for today's walk) and myself. So there is much reminiscing and poking the entrails of the past as we walk to Culcheth Linear Park, which lies on a section of the former Wigan to Glazebrook Railway Line.

For many years, Septimus has been attempting, without success, to find an old boyhood friend. Today there is progress with this search, because Gerry knows the missing person and has more recent knowledge of his whereabouts and contact details. Septimus is delighted.

At Culcheth Gerry hands us over to Ken Critchley. Ken hands us a small envelope with a donation from Jack Delve, who is a volunteer at the park. Jack appears and I have the chance to thank him. He has come specially to open the toilets for us, at the rangers' cabin, which is on the site of the old railway station. Septimus takes advantage of this but is not at all pleased to find that Jack's Rottweiler has followed him to the facilities and blocks his exit.

Ken, who lost his best friend to pancreatic cancer five years ago, shepherds us to the Leeds-Liverpool Canal and on to the Dover Lock pub. Shortly before we arrive at Dover Lock, we meet a friend of Ken's on the canal bank. This is Andy Ling, who is surrounded by a posse of springer spaniels, all marvellously well trained and well behaved. We can hardly help noticing Andy's footwear. He has a Wellington boot on one foot and a walking boot on the other. This is due to an injured foot. Or maybe it is just to provoke conversation. Or perhaps he is a high jumper.

We arrive at Dover Lock, where we are ensconced until tomorrow morning on the pub car park. It is interesting to note that not only are there no bluebirds over, there is no lock here. There was once, but subsidence destroyed it and, to maintain the water levels, locks were built elsewhere. Ken has already pointed out several places alongside the canal which were once upon a time at the same level as the canal bank but which are now several feet below. All this as a result of coalmining, which until recent times was widespread in this area.

Today's walk was short, at 19.5 kms. I am pretty sure I have no long walks left to do. The total for VBW so far is 1760.5 kms As the young man in yesterday's pub would say – Bloody Hell!

At the Dover Lock we have a photo session with the Wigan Observer, have a chat with two cyclists who are doing Lands End to John o'Groats, eat our evening meal in the pub as a thank-you to the landlord (although this is not a condition of him allowing us to camp overnight in his carpark), and have a good night's sleep trying not to worry about the rats, ferrets and mink which we have been warned may nibble our wiring.

Day 66. Dover Lock to Duxbury.

As usual for the past 8 or 9 days, we awake to the drumming of rain on the roof. Unusually, the rain stops as I set out at 7 am. Even more unusually, there is no more rain during the walk.

I walk alone for 6 kms along the Leigh Branch of the Leeds and Liverpool Canal. At the junction where it meets the main line, near Wigan Pier, I meet Frank Dawber, the founder and leader of the Walters Walking Club. He has told me to look out for a 6 feet 4 inch, good looking sort of fellow. I can confirm that he is tall.

Soon after meeting, we walk up the Wigan Flight of 21 locks. These extend over about 2 miles and are regarded as a bit of a test of a narrowboat captain's logistical skills. Not to mention as a decent morning's exercise. At the top of the flight we chat with a couple who are waiting to take their boat down in the company of a more experienced driver. He tells us about his boat, which is longer than it was. The extension was carried out by the surprisingly simple method of taking the boat out of the water onto a stand, sawing it in two, inserting another section, and welding it all together again.

Frank and I walk on, both in good company, to Duxbury, near Adlington, south of Chorley, where Gay is waiting for us. A nice cup of tea in V-Force One, then Frank sets off for home and we drive to yet another farm campsite, where we are located in a field very close to the M61 motorway.

There is some uncertainty about the arrangements for meeting my next pair of Walters, Clive and Ian. Clive, who actually popped up to greet Ken and me on the towpath today, is not a well man. He suffers badly from asthma, which particularly disables him first thing in the morning.

Distance covered. 20.5 kms. 1780.5 to date. 4 more days to go.

Ferlin Husky sang a song with the title "My home town". It started "I'm wondering if anyone remembers me, in my home town".

That line has been running through my head lately.

My home town is Blackpool, and I have been walking towards it for 66 days now. It is, I can assure you, a very long way from where I live, especially travelling on Shanks' Pony. I have rarely read of anyone walking so far, and never anybody 70 years of age.

I am receiving huge support in the way of blog readership, encouraging comments and e-mails, and donations to my chosen cause, Pancreatic Cancer UK. This support comes from all over Britain and all over the world. But not from Blackpool.

Blackpool was the birthplace and final home of Gaile, my late first wife, in whose name is the fund associated with my walk. She was related to several illustrious footballers in the glorious past of Blackpool Football Club – providing a link between my walk and this year's triumphant return of Blackpool to top-flight football.

And yet there have been more donations to the fund from New Zealand than from Blackpool. More from the United States. More from Italy.

There have been scores of donations, which, as of today, have taken the fund to 87% of the target of £7,000. Only two contributions have been from Blackpool.

I find this very disappointing. Or maybe the people of Blackpool have a penchant for teasing, saving it all for a last-minute rush?

Day 67. Duxbury to Preston.

At last night's campsite there was one other campervan in the field. We didn't even see the people belonging to it. They weren't there when we arrived and when the campervan came back we never saw anybody get out of it. But it was lashing down with rain more or less from soon after we parked until we went to bed. It is still raining a bit this morning. I don't know what happened to the drought which brought about a hosepipe ban.

Gay has driven me down from Adlington to Skew Bridge, Bridge 72a on the Leeds-Liverpool Canal. I now have to walk 6 kms on my own to Bridge 81, where I should meet Clive and Ian, today's Walters, at 8 am. Then I believe at some stage between there and Preston, Ian's wife is supposed to join us, possibly with another woman who can then drive her home. They are taking me to Preston. From Preston I will find the Lancaster Canal and walk up that a few kms to where Gay and I have identified a picking-up spot, which is a sports stadium. The reason for selecting that is that it should be somewhere easy for Gay to park.

Things do not go to plan. The Walters are not at Bridge 81. I wait for almost half an hour then walk on up the canal. Gay and I have not worked out a route because we are supposed to be marching to the sound of the Walters' drum. I have a feeling I am heading in the wrong direction and indeed I am.

I have gone a few kms when Clive 'phones me (I had tried to 'phone him but had been given the wrong number). He has been delayed. I walk back to a new rendezvous. There are some further difficulties in liaison before I meet Clive, Ian and Ian's wife at the entrance to the Cuerden Valley Park, which is on the other side of the A6 road, two hours after the appointed time.

Unfortunately, Clive immediately has to drop out because he is suffering badly from his asthma. Ian's wife stays to look after Clive, and Ian Smith guides me through the Cuerden Valley Park, over the River Ribble and into the heart of Preston. Ian is another one who knows how dreadful pancreatic cancer is because he lost his mother to the illness.

By the time we reach Preston I am keen to stop for a drink but we are already well behind schedule and it is still raining heavily. Rather than waste more time walking into the shopping centre for a decent café, Ian and I stop off at a sandwich shop which also provides takeaway drinks. There are a couple of tables with chairs outside. They are wet, but so are we, so we perch awhile, consuming the coffees and my blueberry muffin. Then we head off to find the start of the Lancaster Canal. Just as we are negotiating today's only noisy bit of road, near the docks, I receive a call from BBC television, who intend to be at the finish on Friday, but want to check the time and place. The roar of traffic at a busy junction means that it is impossible to converse. They say they will ring again later, but do not. When we reach the Lancaster canal, Ian departs while I walk a further 3 kms to find Gay waiting at the Preston Sports Arena, a huge complex by the side of the canal.

I had intended to make a nostalgia detour to Lancaster Road in Preston, but the day had been long, with two completely wasted hours, and the rain was very wet. So I gave it the go-by.

But Lancaster Road played a big part in my life. It is where the Northern Counties Wireless School was based. So keen was I to start the seafaring life, that I insisted on leaving grammar school at 15, to attend radio school and qualify as a radio officer. It was a very foolish thing to do – the sea would probably have waited for me – but my life seems to have worked out OK despite the truncated school years and the lack of those basic qualifications (I did acquire others).

The NCWS premises were over Watson and Wrigley's workwear clothing shop. I commuted there for fifteen months, travelling sometimes by train, sometimes by bus. The school was run by an eccentric Irishman, but most of the course work was taken by a lecturer who knew his stuff but didn't know how to control a room full of unruly young men. He particularly couldn't handle it when they were pulling his leg.

Some of the students used to go to the Golden Cross pub nearby, where you could get pie, chips and peas, plus a half-pint of Watney's Red Barrel for 2 shillings at lunchtime. There was also Mrs Bolton's café round the corner at the market – this provided cheap meals which would keep a body and soul together with bacon butties and the like until one could escape to sea and the usually excellent meals in the officer's dining rooms.

As with my school chums, I have some difficulty remembering the names of my Radio College colleagues, although I can visualise some of them quite well. They were all older than me. Some were using the college to train for a change of career. At least one of those had been in the army.

One person, who I remember as "Ginger" had been a steward in the Merchant Navy and wanted to improve his lot. Like many stewards he either had or affected an effeminate manner. He had "seen it all" in his years at sea and loved to shock the less experienced among us by lurid tales of sexual shenanigans abroad or at sea, or by pretending (I assume) to make a play for "a nice young boy". Ginger was also a Teddy Boy – for this was their heyday – and affected drape jackets, drainpipe trousers, "brothel-creeper" shoes and a DA haircut. He lived in Blackpool so we frequently travelled together. This meant I sometimes saw him with his guard down, worrying about his future and his relationships. Something I have noticed all my life is that the brasher people seem to be, the more vulnerable and insecure they are when you get to know them. Ginger wasn't an extreme example of this type, but he was an early lesson to me that what you see in people isn't necessarily what is there.

After Gay picks me up we high-tail it to Lytham, where the fourth attempt at receiving Gay's replacement Visa card is foiled because, despite long discussions on the telephone and clear directions to the bank, and their agreement, the card has been sent to our home address, where we are not, instead of the HSBC Lytham Branch, where we are, by appointment.

Most of today's walk was through heavy rain. The hosepipe ban in this area has been in force about 10 days, as has the rain.

Distance today was 30 kms, total so far 1810.5 kms.

Day 68. Preston to Garstang.

I have just about dried out today, after yesterday's continuous and intensive downpour. We stayed the night at the extraordinary Great Birchwood Country Park near Lytham, which is a cross between a campsite and a town from the wild west. They have country music and line dancing there at the weekends. We have been intrigued by this place for years. Unfortunately, having now been there, we are none the wiser. The place was a lake, everybody was cowering in their caravans. There was no sign of any staff, we did not even make contact with management, so we came away this morning, guilty, without paying (being of an honest disposition, we contacted them later and sent the money).

Gay drives me back to the huge sports complex in Preston, just off the Lancaster Canal. My son-in-law Kenny is with us. We met Karen and Kenny last night for the first time this year. They live and work in Saudi Arabia and are here especially for the end of VBW. They kindly took us out for a meal last night.

Soon after starting out, Kenny and I see a tree, brought down during the night by the rain, and which is now totally blocking the canal. It is a big tree and will take some shifting. I'm not sure how they will do it – the canal path is hardly designed for heavy lifting gear.

We bowl along the first 16 kms – interrupted only by a telephone interview with Radio Wave in Blackpool – to Guy's Thatched Hamlet at Bilsborrow, where not only is Gay waiting, but so is Nicola with her family, Fabrizio and the two boys Alessandro and Francesco. Again, we have not seen them this year as they live in Italy.

Kenny's diabetes has recently taken a turn for the worse and he has moved onto medication. Karen texts him every 10 minutes to make sure he takes a glucose tablet, but even so, between the start of today's walk and Guy's, his blood count halves.

We have a coffee at Guy's. Before we resume the walk, Kenny borrows their car keys from Karen because he needs to get something. We then set off to complete the other 11 kms of today's walk. We are quite far along from Guy's to the Bridge Marina when Karen 'phones Kenny to say she is sitting at Guy's with the car and Kenny has the car keys in his pocket.

So Nicola has to drive Karen up to our campsite to pick up the keys, and then back again. The Bridge Marina Campsite in Garstang is a lovely site, even without the rabbits which are dodging about all over the place. They are the tamest rabbits we have ever seen.

Today's "route march", as Kenny calls it, was 27 kms. Bringing VBW to 1837.5 kms to date. A few weeks later, when Karen and Kenny are back in Saudi Arabia, they discover that he had a heart attack only a few days before the route march.

In the evening Nicola and family come to the campsite to meet us and we go to the pricey but not particularly good – judging by the pizzas we had – Italian restaurant in Garstang.

Then Nicola is kind enough to drive along most of my route for the following day, to check out whether there are pavements all of the way. The road is pretty busy. She says that in the places where the pavement is missing, there is flat, walkable grass.

Day 69. Garstang to Staining.

I start a bit later than normal because BBC Radio Lancashire, in the shape of Alison Butterworth, comes to interview us at 7 am. We are live on the program. We shall also be on the same radio station, different program, for the big finish tomorrow. Last night I received a message that BBC Look NorthWest, the tv programme, are going to be at the finish. I know a lot of people have been writing to the BBC to tell them this is a human interest story they should be covering. Today we are on the Graham

Liver show. A couple of months later Graham Liver himself will be raising money for charity by cycling to Blackpool from Paris, from the Eiffel Tower to Blackpool Tower.

Today's walk turns out to be much longer than I intended.

I walk from Garstang to, first, a coffee shop in St Michaels, then a coffee shop in Great Eccleston. At the latter there are some people who say they have already passed me while I was walking. We have a chat about what I am doing. They seem very interested. They leave. When it is my turn to go, I find they have paid for my coffee. Then they pass me again while I am walking, slowing almost to a halt, say something encouraging, and zoom off. I don't realise who it is until they are pulling away again so I don't get a chance to say thanks.

Then things take a turn for the worse. I have been misinformed, or perhaps I have not listened properly. Either way, I go several kms past the campsite where Gay is waiting. Also, I receive calls from BBC Radio Lancashire to make arrangements for the morrow, and from BBC TV, who want to come to the campsite tomorrow morning at 9. It is obvious that this would not leave me time to walk to the destination for the appointed finish time of 11 am. So I carry on now and walk to within 2 kms of the finish. Both BBC teams will interview us much nearer to the finish, this should leave me enough time to complete the walk, and all should be hunky-dory.

In this last part of today's hike, I pass Baines' Grammar School, which I attended from 1951 to 1955. In those days, all schoolkids had to take an exam, the 11-plus, to decide whether you would spend the next few years at a grammar school or at what was regarded as a lesser secondary school. With my birthday being at the very end of the academic year, I was 11-minus when I took this exam, and only just turned 11-plus when I started at Baines'.

It was a boys-only school in those days, but for some time now it has been mixed. Not only that, but, like most grammar schools, it was turned into a comprehensive by politicians who thought it was good to level down; to reduce the prospects of the more academically inclined while not much improving the chances of the less gifted; to have factories of mediocrity rather than centres of excellence for improving brighter young minds.

Probably because I moved away from the area at 17, I have rarely since seen any of my contemporaries from the school. I remember little about most of them. But I do remember quite a few of the teachers.

Our French teacher was a real character. H. Ellis Thomlinson, known as "Thos". He was a big wheel in the heraldry world, and was commissioned regularly to produce the coat of arms for a lord, a town, or some other body. Sometimes he would tell us about interesting aspect of heraldry, or about one of his clients. He would also use his artistic skills to draw little cartoons on the blackboard to illustrate some point about the French lesson.

He used to appoint boys to various duties – the "calcitrator" had the honour of wiping chalk from the blackboard whenever required; the "fenestrator's" job was to open or close the windows on command. A bell would sound throughout the main school at the beginning or close of each period, but the first form annexe was not on the circuit. Thos would appoint a "tintinabulator", who, at the appointed time, would be sent into the corridor to ring a handbell. Thos was also my form master in the second year.

Our geography teacher was "Piggy" Moulding and the history teacher was Eric Hood, one of the few teachers who did not seem to warrant a nickname. "Minnie" Mitchell's job was to teach us maths and science.

"Yappy" Yates was the Canadian who took us for PT and Hygiene. On February 6th, 1952, we had just finished a PT lesson. We were all in the changing room at the gym, in various stages of undress, some boys still in the shower. The school secretary, Mr Kirwin, came in and had a quiet word with Yappy (who was of course still dressed, in his white cricket trousers and a white t-shirt – the only t-shirt, at the time, that I had ever seen). They both looked shocked. Mr Kirwin then scurried off to pass the news on to another teacher. Yappy said, "Pay attention, boys. The news has just been announced that King George the Sixth passed away during the night. The King is dead, long live the Queen! You will all now stand to attention, and there will be two minutes silence." Picture the sight of all these eleven and twelve year old boys, standing stock still, some dressed only in their socks; some still naked and shivering under the showers, which had of course been switched off as a sign of respect; some fully or almost dressed. And Yappy, dressed in the pseudo-athletic kit which he donned to watch others take exercise, rigidly at attention and holding in his stomach. Kings and Queens were still taken very seriously in those days.

Gay picks me up and we go back to the campsite, which is an outpost of Blackpool's accommodation requirements and is therefore huge and impersonal.

Gay's sister Dana e-mails from Australia, "I hope you had time to muse on your past life a bit more than your blog entries indicate. Did you come to any revelation or experience any epiphany?" I'm afraid I didn't. I thought that could happen. But in real life I have been too busy trying to make sure I go in the right direction, take photographs, dictate the day's events into the recorder, drink enough water, don't fall over, speak to lots of people, and so on. I have thought no great thoughts. I'm quite disappointed.

I have unexpectedly walked 26.5 kms and the total so far is 1864 kms.

Day 70. Staining to Blackpool.

Gay and I drive to Staining Road End, which is 2 or 3 kms from the finish line. I actually walked a kilometre beyond here yesterday but we are here because there is a pub which has a car park, and therefore has room for our big vehicle and the broadcasters. We install ourselves there and soon Alison from BBC Radio Lancashire arrives and wires us up. She did the same thing yesterday morning before we went on air. We each have a pair of headphones and a small radio – mine fits in my pocket. This is so we are aware of what is happening on the programme. My scheduled arrival time stated two years ago is 11 am. Alison wants me to arrive a few minutes early so that she can interview me before the programme finishes at 11 am. She briefs me on how I should coordinate my arrival with other things happening at the finish.

Elaine Dunkley arrives from BBC TV, Look NorthWest. Alison drives off to Bardsway Avenue. Elaine has arrived without the members of her camera crew because they have been diverted to a fire at a motorway service station. So she will have to do the filming as well as interviewing. She interviews Gay and myself, films me shaking hands with a man who comes across from the shops to speak to me. She films me putting on my shoes. I receive a text message from my granddaughter Alexandra. Elaine films me reading it aloud. Then she has me marching up and down in front of the shops, crossing roads, coming round corners. She fixes me up with a clip on microphone to be used when I arrive. Then she is off in her car, following Gay who is driving V-Force One.

For some time now I have been catching glimpses of Blackpool Tower, which thrusts toward the sky a couple of miles away. I mentioned earlier that my home stands in the shadow of Puivert Castle, which was the last thing I saw as I set out on Day One. My first home was similarly dominated by Blackpool Tower. For the first 17 years of my life I saw it every time I went in or out of the house.

Like me and the walk, it has a French connection. The idea for the tower was born when Blackpool businessman and councillor John Bickerstaffe visited the Great Paris Exhibition in 1889. He saw the Eiffel Tower and thought it would look very nice on Blackpool seafront and would attract many visitors, all eager to spend their money in his town.

Unfortunately, the Eiffel Tower was not for sale so Mr Bickerstaffe and some chums drummed up a committee, then a company, then some finances, some designers, lots of steel and piles of bricks. They set about making a copy of the Eiffel Tower. They were not very ambitious because instead of making a tower bigger and better than the Eiffel, they made a half-size copy, although it did contain a zoo, a circus and a spectacular ballroom in the building which surrounded the base. I was always very impressed with the fact that the design included a wobble factor, so that it would sway in the wind, instead of resisting and being snapped off. I was even more impressed that, in the event of trouble, there was a bias for the tower to flop into the Irish Sea instead of into the town, where it would interrupt the free-spending of holidaymakers.

As I walk along I am listening to the Ted Robbins programme in my headphones. He is interviewing various people in the studio, between playing some records. At about 10.45 he brings in Alison, who by then is standing outside the house where I was born. There is a bit of a crowd of people who have come to witness the finish to Vic's Big Walk. I hear Karen and Nicola being interviewed. They say that it probably means more to them than anybody else because I am walking, and raising funds, in the name of their mother. My brother Christopher is asked if I have always been "sporty". He says I am the only person he ever knew who used to score goals by heading the ball when it was on the ground.

I am not sure what my thoughts and feelings would otherwise have been as I approach the end of this long march, and the place of my birth and childhood, but I am diverted by my need to stick to Alison's schedule. I am supposed to appear around the corner just as she says, "I wonder where Vic is now – let's go to the top of the street to see if he is in sight". As she says, there is nothing contrived in broadcasting. Timing it right is difficult and by 10.45 I am within 100 yards. I skulk first at the top of Ingleway, then at the top of Fordway. These streets, together with Bardsway Avenue and a couple of others, are on one of the few hills in Blackpool. We used to whizz down the hills on skateboards, which in those days were just short boards balanced on roller skates.

I get the timing right and come round the corner of Bardsway Avenue to find Alison and Gay a few yards from me, coming to see, in a broadcast sort of fashion, if I am nearby. Gay kisses me, I think Alison does too. They each grab an arm and shepherd me down the street.

Gay has managed to park V-Force One right outside the house, which is amazing. It is a narrow street, not built for much traffic and normally it has cars parked nose to tail on each side. Alison's radio van is there as well, and Elaine's car. Elaine films my approach. There are friends from my youth and others from more recent times, two of my brothers with their wives, Karen and Kenny, and Nicola, Fabrizio, Alessandro and Francesco from Italy. What really takes me by surprise is that the current occupant of the house has decorated it with banners wishing me a happy 70th birthday. Some months earlier I had called at the house to warn this lady that there may be a commotion outside it, a possible crowd, maybe with radio and tv people. I thought she had not absorbed what I told her, or maybe she thought I was some conman trying to get into the house. But Sharon has really risen to the occasion. She is friendly and helpful, happy to let Alison take me inside the house and ask me how I feel – to be frank it is all a bit of a blur.

The spot where I am standing when Alison asks me how I feel is where my father's chair used to be. We didn't see a lot of my father during the week, because he was up and out before we got up, he worked a long day, came home, ate his dinner then went to sleep. When he awoke, or on occasion as a bonus before he went to sleep, he would sometimes let us tickle his feet and marvel that this didn't make him squirm, as it did when he tickled us. Or he would let us examine the hole in his cheek where he had had a cyst removed and where he said he kept his money. Another place he kept money was in the wide money belt which, along with his braces, held up his trousers. He also kept mice in there, he told us. In fact there were probably more mice in there than pound notes. He was poorly paid and there can't have been much left after feeding and clothing a large family. It is surprising that he could afford to smoke, but he did so. He used to save the "dog ends" in a tin box. When there were enough to justify the effort, we all used to tear them apart, throw away the paper, then my father would make new cigarettes using the second hand tobacco and a little Rizla cigarette roller.

Both my father and my mother were very fond of singing and music. They had a gramophone which had to be wound up before each record was played. The needles were metal or wood and had to be changed regularly, if not for every record. Sometimes the gramophone slowed in mid-record and somebody had to leap to it and crank the mechanism so that Kathleen Ferrier didn't sound like Paul Robeson. The records were of "real" singers, particularly Irish tenors like Josef Locke and John McCormack. My parents had a horror of "crooners" like Bing Crosby and Frank Sinatra, and of "street singers" like Vera Lynn.

Other musical entertainment was provided by my father playing a small organ which was somehow squeezed into the living room, while we all gathered round and sang rousing songs, which were frequently hymns or had some religious content.

Then there was the radio. There was no such thing as television in those days, except for a favoured few. The first tv broadcasts were a couple of years before I was born, and only in the London area. I certainly knew nobody who had television when I was small. In fact I had never heard of it. But radio entertainment was very common. That's where the news came from, although it was only every few hours, not every thirty minutes, as it is these days. There were also a lot of situation comedies such as "Ray's a Laugh", which consisted of a series of small sketches, utilising the same characters each week, in different stories, but always with the same catch phrases and punch lines. It sounds ridiculous, but it worked, and kept a large chunk of the nation entertained for years.

The number of radio stations was very limited. There were the three BBC stations: the Light Programme (comedy and music for the masses), the Third Programme (very highbrow and not approved of at Heaney Towers, although this is presumably where one would have found Kathleen Ferrier and Gigli) and the Home Service (news and other serious matters). There was certainly no Radio Lancashire.

Since my mother left it to go into a nursing home about ten years ago, the house has been modernised. Everything has changed. I don't know if Sharon still has a clock, as my father did, which operated on relative time. His clock would lose several minutes a day but, instead of correcting it, he would note how many minutes slow it was. It could be more than half an hour wrong and you had to know today's margin of error and add it to the decoy time displayed by the clock. Such odd things comprise the memories of childhood.

Both Alison and Elaine interview me some more. Champagne appears. Karen and Nicola are holding a wonderful cake which Karen has made – an exact, but unfortunately smaller replica of V-Force One, even down to precise copies of the Columbia and Satmap logos, the Vic's Big Walk logo and the URL of my blog. All eatable.

We mill around for a while. Sharon kindly lets me have a look at my old bedroom, except that it is not there. The first door at the top of the stairs, which is where my bedroom was, now leads into the bathroom. The remainder of what was the bedroom has been merged with what was the bathroom to form the bedroom of Sharon's son. I am pleased to see that he has a guitar. It is still a two bedroom house, as it was when my mother and father raised five boys there. At one time we had my mother's sister and her baby boy living with us as well. I have no memory of how we all managed to fit in, or where we all slept. My first memory is of being woken up by a baby's cry. This was the night my brother Paul, also known as Septimus, who has walked 4 days with me during VBW, was born. It may be a coincidence that on the same date Adolf Hitler committed suicide.

There is a call for Elaine on my Blackberry. The news item, which was scheduled for the evening news, is now required at lunchtime. Elaine has to get her skates on with the editing, ready to hand over to a despatch rider.

The local press is here as well, in the form of a very pushy photographer. The Blackpool Gazette has already published three items about my walk and another one is scheduled about the finish. And yet still there has been very little response from the people of this town, either in support or donations to the fund for Pancreatic Cancer UK. Maybe they can sense that although I was born here, I am not a Blackpool man. I have not been walking "home". I have been walking from my home to this place where I happened to start my life.

I remain in Blackpool for less than two hours. A number of us go for lunch to Tiffins in the old windmill complex at Thornton. Then we move on to Guy's, which Kenny and I called at during our walk 2 days ago. This is about 20 kms from Blackpool. There is a slap-up dinner arranged for tonight with family and friends. Samantha and Matthew surprise me by turning up. Since the beginning of the year, Samantha has been living in Boston, Massachusetts. I knew she was in Germany on business but had no idea she was intending to be here. So all my daughters are here from their far-flung diaspora. Matthew's presence means that all my grandchildren are present, except for Joshua, who is visiting his girlfriend's family in California. Alexandra, although not at the finish line, will be here for tonight's celebrations. We shall be seeing Joshua before we leave the country.

Before going for dinner in the evening, we all make sure to watch Look North

West on TV. The BBC have had the last word about a theme tune for Vic's Big Walk – they play Walk of Life, by Dire Straits. I couldn't have made a finer choice myself.

The walk is over. I am very close to my fundraising target and will soon surpass it. The amount raised is a drop in the ocean of what is needed to defeat pancreatic cancer, but it is a contribution, nevertheless. Perhaps more importantly, I have helped to raise awareness of this appalling plague and the need for some progress. I have spoken to scores, possibly hundreds of people about it. My blog has been seen by many thousands. Media coverage has reached far wider.

On a more personal level, the fact that I have undertaken this huge walk in memory of their mother has cemented and deepened my already excellent relationship with Karen and Nicola.

A week in Scotland, with Karen and Kenny, Nicola, Fabrizio, Alessandro and Francesco, starts tomorrow. So does the rest of my life, which may now be more normal than the past 70 days. I am pleased, in a way, that the BBC did not choose "On the Road Again". No, I am not walking back to France. Not yet, anyway.

Kilometres walked today – 3. Total for the whole walk, brought down by Gay's excellent planning from a possible 2,000 or more, was 1867 kms.

I raised, together with the contribution for the taxman, over £10,000 for pancreatic cancer research. Your purchase of this book has increased that. A donation, however small, would increase it further.

Photographs can be seen at:
https://picasaweb.google.com/vicngay/VicSBigWalk02

—

My blog is ongoing and can be found at:
http://vicsbigwalk.blogspot.com

—

All proceeds of this book are going direct to pancreatic cancer research and you can still donate to Pancreatic Cancer UK at:
http://www.justgiving.com/Vic-Heaney/

—

The BBC News on TV - dubbed by others Vic's Big Walk - The Movie – can be found at:
http://www.youtube.com/watch?v=oXEsgaK8EL0

—

Enjoyed this book?

3 more Vic Heaney books will be published, in both e-book and paperback, during 2012 and 2013:

Living on an Island - Cyprus is about the 8 years Vic and Gay spent living on that Mediterranean island.

Swim the Atlantic? is a collection of memories from Vic's long and interesting life.

Vic's Shorts is a selection of the many short stories Vic has written for competition entries - at least 5 of them having been shortlisted.